I0821773

THE BLACK BOOK II

THE BLACK BOOK II

FROM HAJJI MALIK AL-SHABAZZ TO BARACK OBAMA

DR. Y. N. KLY

CLARITY PRESS, INC.

ISBN: 0-932863-88-4
978-0-932863-88-1

In-house editor: Diana G. Collier
Cover: R. Jordan P. Santos
Illustration: Arvie Villena

Library of Congress Cataloging-in-Publication Data

Kly, Yussuf Naim, 1935-
The black book II : from Hajji Malik al-Shabazz to Barack Obama / Y.N. Kly.
p. cm.
ISBN-13: 978-0-932863-88-1
ISBN-10: 0-932863-88-4
1. X, Malcolm, 1925-1965--Political and social views. 2. King, Martin Luther, 1899-1984--Political and social views. 3. Obama, Barack--Political and social views. 4. Black nationalism--United States. 5. African American politicians. 6. African Americans--Politics and government. 7. United States. President (2009- : Obama) I. Title.

BP223.Z8.L576K59 2010
320.54'6092--dc22

Clarity Press, Inc.
Ste. 469, 3277 Roswell Rd. NE
Atlanta, GA. 30305, USA
http://www.claritypress.com

TABLE OF CONTENTS

OBSERVATION

John Locke has been widely revered in the teaching of American history as one of the thinkers of the European Enlightenment. However, viewing him from "The Dark Side"—the African American perspective—Locke was one of the founders of domestic colonialism in America. He was a major investor in the English slave-trade through the Royal African Company, as well as through his participation in drafting the *Fundamental Constitution of the Carolinas* while Shaftesbury's secretary, which established a feudal aristocracy and gave his so-called master absolute power over his so-called slaves. As a secretary to the Council of Trade and Plantations (1673–4) and a member of the Board of Trade (1696–1700) *Locke was, in fact, "one of just half a dozen men who created and supervised both the colonies and their iniquitous systems of servitude".** *As such, his opposition to slavery in his major writings was clearly hypocritical. His notion of liberty related only to the freedom of English capitalists to exploit. His statements on unenclosed property are viewed as having justified the displacement of the Native Americans.*

That Locke continues to be widely viewed as a beacon of enlightenment in America demonstrates how the writing of history in the United States does not reflect the perspective of "one-state, one-nation" but merely the perspective of the dominant Anglo-American majority.

This book seeks to address the problematic of the blending of the incompatibilities between the notions of "enlightenment", and the actualities of enslavement, domestic colonialism and imperialism into a unique American concept of democracy.

* Martin Cohen, *Philosophical Tales,* (Blackwell 2008, p. 101)

OBSERVATION TWO

Political science can be said to be only a small part of religion or non-religious philosophy. If we put all of Hajji Malik Al-Shabazz's presentations into an appropriate political framework, we find that although he did not finish his educational training, he was a great political thinker. One comes to understand that Hajji Malik Al-Shabazz did not believe that the US political system could be sufficiently changed without struggle. (Unlike the many who want to go to heaven, few are willing to die for it…) During the last days of Hajji Malik's life, we were told by members of the OAAU (his bodyguards) how Hajji Malik Al-Shabazz stepped forward without sufficient bodyguards because he felt it was best for the benefit of African American liberation. Hajji Malik believed that God helps those who help themselves, or "Surely, Allah changes not the condition of a people until they change themselves", Qur'an, Sura Al-Rad, ayat 11.

Perhaps different from Dr. Martin Luther King, Jr. or Barack Obama, he seems to have had no illusions about the American government system and how it would resist change, Thus Hajji Malik was great, not just because he was right, but also because he took pleasure in learning, and had the courage and integrity to reject anything he or his people did not feel was right. By any means necessary. Because of Hajji Malik, African Americans will shelter in the light. (After taking his wife, Sister Betty, to the New Moon Chinese restaurant shortly after his assassination, it was clear to us that their fire would remain even without a flame, and the guiding light for a new path to African American liberation from domestic colonialism had only been successfully delayed.)

After the assassination came the flyers by night (the House Negroes) each seeking with the help of their position in the Anglo-American pecking order as well as that of the African American community, to get whatever was left: the jobs, etc. that his name brought into existence. They restored his ancient automobile, but neglected his ideas and fail to mention the most important of his learning experiences, his trip to Mecca.

Hajji Malik Al-Shabazz' understanding of the American system was as clear as that of any great political scientist such as Gabriel Almond.* This is why he appears to have understood the role of political parties, the House Negro, forced assimilation, propaganda, etc. within the US system. This is why he knew that to achieve the desired change, he would have to provide for the intervention of international human rights law.

*Hajji Malik understood how a political system is made up of institutions, such as interest groups, political parties, the executive, legislative and judicial branches of government, and a bureaucratic machinery, and that interest groups serve to articulate political issues; parties then aggregate and express them in a coherent and meaningful way for the masses to address the majority interests. However, even those systems where the majority interest is uniquely addressed are never entirely self-contained; they exist in a dynamic relationship to other political systems and must continuously adapt to changing conditions in the larger information law (human rights law). This is one of the reasons that all systems can be changed by international cooperation with the struggles for human rights. Hajji Malik realized by his actions that the dominant majority controlled political socialization, the process by which a culture passes down civic values, beliefs, and habits of mind to succeeding generations. *It is largely an unconscious process by which families, schools, communities, political parties and other agents of socialization inculcate the culture's dominant* Anglo-American *politi*cal values. All recruitment of citizens is largely an unconscious process by which they become active participants in the political system. He viewed the reason for and role of the House Negro within this context *The US government, like all governments, has inherent biases or normative implications. First, it is by its very nature conservative. Hajji Malik Al-Shabazz recognized that a political system's first objective is to ensure its own survival, and that all political actors, black or white, and institutions within that system, are essentially used to assist or maintain the survival of that system. For this reason, it is not especially responsive to innovations and movements aimed at political change—that is, beyond those that strengthen its adaptiveness and resilience.*

OBSERVATION THREE

African Americans were kidnapped in Africa and brought to the New World, where they were inflicted with cruel, inhuman and unnatural treatment, and endured an absolute terrorism which was expected to force them into becoming voluntary slaves of their kidnappers.

This was not a natural occurrence but a well-planned wicked experiment that used every form of mental, physical and sociological torture to achieve its objectives—such as forcing our Aunts to drop their babies into the fireplace because they were not wanted by their fathers. This was among the kinds of wicked and criminal acts for which no reconciliation in the manner proposed by President Obama can make amends or satisfy states' obligations to provide redress for human rights violations.

Insofar as U.S. law is subservient to international law, this may require not just an apology but compensation, restitution, or rehabilitation for grave violations of human rights and fundamental freedoms.*

*Commission on Human Rights resolution 2003/34, <http://www.unhchr.ch/huridocda/huridoca.nsf/(Symbol)/E.CN.4.RES.2003.34.En?Opendocument>

Introduction

The western world continues to lose its global leadership status due to its inability to institutionalize and take seriously the ideals, etc. that it, itself, has been so instrumental in developing and protecting. The Anglo-American empire[1] continues to struggle for the maintenance of what one might call domestic colonialism[2] in the new world (North America) and a new American form of neo-imperialism in developing states. Even after the legitimacy and practice of western European international colonization and imperialism has dimmed, the US policies and politic can be considered to result from what advocates of the "American Century" may consider the more successful colonialist model for global political hegemony through the tactic and model of "domestic colonialism". Not only did the US model lead to politico-economic success, but it did so despite the fact that this success depended heavily on the US attempts at enslavement of captured Africans and the near ethnocide of the indigenous populations.

In modern history, however, the American model has been so successful at hiding under the banner of democracy that the world had come to view the US as the best hope for the protection of democracy, human rights, good governance, sustainable development, and war against global poverty. The most insightful writings of V.T. Rajshekar (as often appearing in the Bangalore bi-monthly, *Dalit Voice*[3]), which advise that for any of these hopes to be realized, the situation of the oppressed must be framed within the context of the struggle of nations within states to achieve social, cultural and economic equal status (collective or individual self-determination)[4] merit our serious consideration. Otherwise, such hopes can be only for the few (the ruling classes).[5]

The neo-colonialism and neo-imperialism of domestic colonialism becomes most visible when observing the unique weaknesses of the economic, political and social institutions historically evolved for the equal status protection of peoples such as African-Americans, First Nations, Dalits, Roma, Kashmiris, etc. in the USA, India and elsewhere. All these political institutions and the socio-political philosophies that support them seem designed to forcibly incorporate or maintain such peoples into political units that are under the jurisdiction of descendants of the original European colonists or dominant (Brahmin) ruling majority, etc., who they seem to feel would keep them at the bottom of the pecking order and without socio-cultural equal status.[6]

Thus, the problematic of such systems is not only caused by economic factors, but equally by socio-cultural and political factors that operate to prevent or fail to find a way to provide socio-political and economic equal status to such groups, nations, communities or peoples by not providing them with their human rights, particularly their most important human right to self-determine so that they too can achieve equal status development. Instead, such governments prefer to see all issues from the point of view of the will of the majority, and encourage the development of political concepts that may exploit and damage the development potential of their minorities (particularly those minorities unsure of their internationally protected personalities).

While traditional colonialism profits from capitalism and imperialism, domestic colonialism seems to be more *parasitical*—in the sense that both the victim and the host are parties to the same state, which provides greater access for the purposes of exploitation to all aspects of the daily life skills and needs of the victim. We suggest that states like the US which practice domestic colonialism have better access to their victims for exploitation, making that exploitation less costly, and more efficient and effective. Thus self-determination, self-definition, and the right to be different is discouraged or blocked. The problematic for states becomes how to disguise, under the banner of democracy, a cultural, political and economic system that will permit this effective and efficient exploitation. In situations involving states and national minorities, it is politically fair to remember that a parasite cannot live alone. If the relationship between the majority and minorities is parasitic for whatever reason, the parasite, in order to exist, will need, for whatever reason, to maintain the existing status of the host in order to maintain its own status and identity. Historically it is important to take into consideration the fact that the US and much of the Anglo-American empire is different from most states in that t*he United States is not a nation seeking to become a state, but a state seeking to create a nation.*

There is need for further research on the significance of the above as it relates to parasitic imperialism/domestic colonialism, and how this history influences US domestic and foreign policy. In such regard, the US policies of permanent US Congressional trusteeship under the legal control of the Minister of the Interior and Congress without democratic consent as it concerns the indigenous Americans, or forced assimilation without seeking the collective consent of the African Americans, etc., merit special notice. The placement of the German Americans in Midwestern states by Roosevelt, the use of Chinese Americans to build railroads, the internship of the Japanese Americans during the second world war, etc.—the effort to divide the nation into white, black and others who are still all "the same"—provide reasons to re-examine the nature of the type of nations that the Anglo-American elites are attempting to create.

Are these policies and their supporting institutionalized practices a sincere and democratic attempt to provide for the successful integration of all ethnic and minority communities into one (a new, single-nation state), or do they simply permit and encourage a type of what we will call parasitic relation between the dominant group and minorities, particularly the national minority. As the solution to the problematic posed by European powers competing for stakes in the new world, the Anglo colonists' elites gave all European (so-called white) Americans a way to share in the booty of the exploitation of the nations (become national minorities) of the Americas. In essence, the ruling elites of the Anglo-American empire have always used their values and political circumstances to orientate and create the kind of nation that suits the "raison d'etre" for European immigration to the lands of the Americas.

Needless to say, this is not the way that Europe and most other developed multinational countries are attempting to deal with themselves in order to achieve unity in diversity. Today the European and other developing states attempt to follow the various interpretations of Article 27 of the International Covenant on Civil and Political Rights, as well as Article 1 of both International Covenants.[7]

Providing for a national minority's equal status international protection in the Americas, particularly in the US, remains difficult because it opposes the American Dream of so many immigrants who choose to come to live in the Americas to enjoy such exploitation. In the past, Europeans and many other immigrants to the US, and indeed to the Americas, have expected a socio-political and economic environment favoring European and other so-defined white elites' exploitation of the land, the resources of the indigenous nations, and the cheap labor and cultural product (entertainment) from the forced African immigrants. To what degree is this still an important draw to the Americas, not only for European immigration today, but for the empire's allies and ruling elites of the world in general? In Europe and the world in general, *there remains an old dream of the new world that will be difficult to revamp.*

The Cold War idea of the "free world" could also have connotations of a free hand to exploit the "new" world for the auto-perpetuation of western civilization in relation to challenges from other civilizations and civilizational socio-political and economic ideologies. As an instance, note the Islamic understanding that was highlighted subsequent to the Iranian peaceful revolution: that both west and east, north and south belong to Allah, but justice as a moral and religious obligation will remain the bar, requiring reconciliation and redress for success.

The Contribution of Western Civilization

While we may understand that everything that humanity calls science is not necessarily true, western civilization has nonetheless helped to solidify the role of the search for true science and most particularly the scientific method in the international hierarchy of belief among the ruling class of the world, just as it has analyzed, evaluated, legalized and prioritized such socio-political ideas as democracy and human rights from the religious philosophies and what are called concepts of natural law. Western civilization (presently led by many peoples of the Anglo-American empire) also brokered some of the most important ideas for cooperative, peaceful and sustainable social development. No matter how these concepts (like the fundamental concept of wearing clothes) are reformed or understood by different cultural and civilizational input, concepts like human rights and democratic decision making and participation will probably never be ignored by future civilizations.

However, it is even more amazing that the leading US state of the Anglo-American empire has brokered these concepts, ideals and the orientation above mentioned, without committing itself (seriously institutionalizing in its actual governance) to any of these concepts. The US fosters the modern concepts as embodied in the Universal Declaration of Human Rights, the UN and international law without any fixed intention to abide by their legal and philosophic norms and rules if they are not in the transitory interest of its administration—like the beautiful flower that has attracted the fly, then become a Venus fly-trap. The key concepts influencing the modus operandi of the Anglo-American empire remain, simply: "pragmatism", "survival of the fittest", "profitability", "capitalism" and perhaps "chosen people".

The problematic of the Anglo-American empire, as before mentioned, lies in its inability to realize or become serious about the fulfillment of its ideals within the context of other competing socio-political and economic interests. This problematic is made visible when we compare the US rhetoric (words) with its deeds (its politico-social and economic policies). These deeds often attempt to hide a double-standards discrimination that can only be related to the pragmatic, immoral and perhaps illegal philosophy of survival of the fittest as it relates to military hegemony. The fact that the realization of ideals would also affect self interest as well as the collective survival chances of the state or empire does not seem to be under serious consideration. The limitation of the necessary policy scope leads to double standards. So the empire speaks of human rights: human rights yes, but for whom? Democracy yes, but defined only in ways that would not threaten the profit motive or the exploitive capacities of the various allied capitalist ruling elites.

Thus American civilization, as epitomized by the CNN News Channel, is always "singing to the choir"—in other words, speaking only to those who believe in the Anglo-American empire and its associated socio-economic and political paradigms—because these are the sole paradigms within which all debate is constrained. It has become arrogant, stagnant, and unable or unwilling to learn from the successful and unsuccessful experience of the other civilizations.

Had western civilization just corrected the term "slaves" to "captured Africans" whom it attempted to enslave—rather than integrating the past mistakes into a future misunderstanding—and addressed the question of redress for their kidnapping, this African/

slave theme in the Anglo-American empire might not have become hardwired but rather become a defining feature of its civilization. Instead this lack of an appropriate apology and redress has created an unworkable contradiction when attempting to define its contribution to human rights and democracy, not only in relation to Americans but also to Africans and the rest of the non-European world in general, who also have absorbed the effects of this abnormality.

African Americans as a collective never accepted enslavement. They fought the effort to enslave them from the time of their arrival as forced immigrants up until today—although the fight against the effort to enslave and the effort to segregate and exploit them took more than a hundred years. (Does the fact that it took 100 years to socio-politically and militarily defeat the effort to enslave African Americans mean that they were slaves? Is it possible to say that the African Americans won the 100-year war against enslavement?) There is no period in African American history in which this fight was absent. Thus the African Americans were the same as those in international colonies, who were colonized and eventually freed themselves. However, while under international colonialism, freedom from the oppressor meant obtaining political independence and led to a continuing struggle against neo-colonialism within the Anglo-American empire, for African Americans, freedom meant obtaining civil rights and then fighting for international recognition of their international personality (collective identity), as part of an ongoing struggle against "domestic colonialism". The currently accepted politically-inspired social history that fails to acknowledge and recognize such understanding has effectively served as a psychological means of helping to keep Africans from eventually achieving equal status with the Anglo-Americans as Founding Fathers of the US who, like the Anglo-Americans, have similar ownership rights to the United States. (If one omits the presence of the indigenous first nations, which of course, we cannot.)

This hardwiring of the American enslavement myth as a part of the political propaganda for purposes of maintainng elite rule of the Anglo-American empire affects other minorities as well, such as Italian-Americans, aboriginal peoples, Spanish Americans, Puerto Ricans, Roma, Serbs, etc. It may have affected an entire stage of the world developmental framework and how that world saw and dealt with the African world—and of course (to a lesser extent) how the African world sees and deals with itself and the Anglo-American empire. At some point, it is probable that Africa has been seen by many people in the world as simply a place where everyone went to get slaves.[8]

The history or problematic of the socio-economic and political developmental diplomacy of Haiti suggests that the diplomacy of countries in Latin America as well as in Europe and elsewhere were impacted by the negative image of Haiti as a so-called slave nation instead of as a nation that had defeated those who had attempted to enslave them. This historical/diplomatic image projected by the US is enough to explain the retardation of Haitian trade and diplomatic development—to say nothing of the fact that the US has actively interfered with and thwarted Haitian relations with other Latin American nations, and initiated regime change. In a similar sense, Haiti's development has been retarded over the 20th century by reparations demanded by France for diplomatic recognition, protection and reparations, regarded as deriving from losses born by France as a result of the liberation of the Haitian people from their enslavement.

What is important to understand is that all people of African descent were gravely hurt and permanently harmed by this propaganda and diplomacy, which was politically necessary to maintain the African enslavement effort in the Americas, and is, along with that of the indigenous nations, perhaps the clearest example of an attempt at genocide directed against a whole continent.

Although the ruling elite of the Anglo-American empire has (intentionally and unintentionally) gravely wronged many peoples, it continues to offer many benefits for global technical and sustainable economic development, although this favorable balance between global benefit and global liabilities seems to be in the process of shifting to the east. This does mean that the Anglo-American empire must lower its guns and abandon a zero/sum future development, thereby accepting policies which permit change along with the need for global equal status development and sustainability. It must open itself to accommodate learning from others' cultures or civilizations as it relates to building a broader philosophical perspective and up-to-date patriotic thematic in which human rights like the right to self-determination (and the abandonment of domestic colonialism) can take new root, and provide for negotiations toward some form of equal-status political autonomy and systemic multinationalism as well as other forms of conflict resolution, fostering the possibility for peaceful global politico-economic development. *In short, stop trying to conquer the world and instead become a dynamic and positive part of it.*

The Cure for Domestic Colonialism

It is significant that the right to self-determination is the first article in borh of the UN international human rights treaties, the ICCPR and the IESCR, because the right to self-define and self-determine, as it might function within the context of a UN Development Assistance Framework (UNDAF), seems to be the only non-violent solution to the question of domestic colonialism. The UNDAF (when done correctly by UN and other personnel) would determine the international legal violations of the minority human rights which the state is legally obligated to correct or redress. If the state is unwilling or unable to respond to its international legal responsibilities, this would raise the right to some form of negotiated self-determination for the national minority. The best example of this in recent times and without the need for the UNDAF was the recent velvet divorce between Czechs and Slovaks in the former Czechoslovakia.

The problematic of domestic colonization as it relates to the colonized inhabitants of North America may still exist today. The question is: does domestic colonialism still remain the marching order of the ruling elites of the Anglo-American empire?

In a situation where aboriginal Canadians and Americans are increasingly accusing their government of finding new ways to unfairly take control of the oil, water, gas and other natural resources on their lands, and of using their political and legal clout to short-change the aboriginal First nations, the Prime Minister of Canada envisages[9] that a future solution will result from the use of indigenous natural resources—a solution which Canadian First Nations might well regard as "doing more of the same thing". In areas where the suicide rate for aboriginal peoples is more than twice the national average,[10] the government ignores what is told to them as the cause of this problem: the sense of hopelessness that results from policies of forced assimilation.[11]

In the meantime, US President Barak Obama seeks to ignore the existence of national minorities and their right to be different, and envisions the future of the USA as being just one nation, one people, one state.[12] Forced assimilation (genocide) is certainly not a new idea. It has already become a human rights violation, over which the International Criminal Court has jurisdiction—as a crime against humanity.

What does this mean in relation to state policies, in the context of the demands of indigenous nations for some type of sovereignty? In what situations and circumstances does it serve the interests of the state (consisting of both majority and minority ethnies) to democratically keep the majority ethny in absolute control of the national minority through the implementation, institutionalization and enforcement of forced assimilation? Why not, like Europe, work to negotiate agreements between governments and national minorities that will permit government to recognize what UNESCO calls the most important human right of all: the democratic right of individuals, minorities and nations to self-determination, without which all other rights have no meaning.[13] Providing for the right to self-determination would, in cases like that of the US, suggest a future multicultural and multinational state instead of the "one state, one nation" model.

As we know, domestic imperialism or colonialism has always involved some form of exploitation or unfair exchange. What Rousseau called "the general will" was interpreted as majority rule when practiced by the US and most of the states of the Anglo-American empire. When practiced in conjunction with a failure to provide for equal status of national minorities, this became "the terror of the majority" or even "the terrorism of the majority".[14]

Is it possible that, having historically chosen to embrace the concept of "the white man's burden" and "manifest destiny" to maintain political control over the national minorities at all costs, the Anglo-American empire's elites steered their ideals and traditional concept of democracy in a contradictory direction—in a direction similar to that of Brahminism as this concerns the Brahmins and the Dalits (and all the castes in between) in what both Indians and Americans persist in calling the largest democracy in the world?

The legacy of the experience of the American colonists with the captured Africans and indigenous peoples, compared with the failure of the European colonial system, allowed the US elites to remind former European powers that only the US techniques of domestic colonialism and imperialism work, and should have been the right political model for white ethnic domination over the non-white ethnies. It is a politico-racial concept of politically transforming and defining all potential power (under the guise of democratic majority rule) as "white"-controlled, which then was to be translated into reality. It has nothing to do with what is needed for the socio-economic development of the largely non-European part of the global village, and if left as the developmental concept of the Anglo-American empire, it would be today simply about eating high on the hog and surviving at the expense of the vulnerable and poor masses of the world.

When the victim and the oppressor are incorporated into one state body, as in the United States, we also call domestic colonialism "domestic parasitism", because it functions like a political virus that robs the victim of his psychic and territorial space as well as control over his daily life, influencing his values and raison d'etre in general, and leading to negative standing across a swathe of social indicators (see Appendix A), including at the far extreme, suicide rates among indigenous populations, as a reflection of their state of hopelessness. It silently eats away at the heart of a peaceful but non-equal status civilization and becomes the seed for future all-out war or collapse of that civilization. It may result from what it may envisage as the successful administration of conquered and oppressed or enslaved nations or the officially recognized conquest of less developed nations entrapped within the territory of a single state.

Domestic or parasitic colonialism requires that its practitioners do the following:

1. Take over the land in such a manner as will permit the conqueror to have a legal right to administer the territory as a part of its domestic territory.
2. Project the perception that the invading power has an overwhelming monopoly of power and cannot be defeated;
3. Institute a constitution which claims to address the needs of all the citizenry for all future generations, regardless of the actual nature and circumstances of the population so aggregated.
4. Inculcate a tendency to view the conquered people as being somehow less than human and make them believe that they will have to become the same as their conquerors in order to be recognized as human beings with human rights.
5. Keep them in an inhuman category without full civil rights until the population of the conqueror becomes the overwhelming majority in the territory of the new state. *Then create a democracy in which the general will imbeds the rule of the majority ethny in all important areas of jurisdiction.*

6. Perpetuate the impression that (somehow) the minority is owned by the conqueror, such as was the case in Haiti and the U.S., etc.
7. Only recognize the equal right to vote of the conquered people after the dominant group has become a numerical majority, created constitutions and founding institutions; and then fail to recognize any right for the minority outside of the parameters of majority rule.
8. Provide the conquered nation with a puppet (House Negro) administration, so-called leaders and leadership from among themselves in order to do the bidding of the conquering nation.
9. Establish such control over the international system as will permit the undemocratic aspects of the conquering state to ignore international norms and rules, thereby providing it with a degree of impunity for almost anything it politically considers a part of its national domestic affairs and foreign interests. (*Gross violation of the human rights of the African American was being practiced in the US at the same time that the US was considered a main proponent of democracy and human rights by many European states and the UN itself.*

Contributions of Hajji Malik Al-Shabazz

Hajji Malik Al-Shabazz, like Martin Luther King, Jr., looked for "peace at last" in the next world (may Allah be pleased with them). But Hajji Malik sought peace of mind in this world as well as in the next. (May Allah be pleased with him.) This meant that people in this world must be able and willing to change their leadership (both Anglo-American and African American) through democratic processes and initiate a sustainable human rights development that can depend on acceptance and negotiation of differences. However, for African Americans and indigenous peoples who were trapped in US domestic colonialism and undergoing forced assimilation to the extent of ethnocide—*unlike for those nations in the West Indies, Africa, Asia, etc—there would be no celebration of political independence, no possibility for free democratic political development that would allow the community to have representatives who would be empowered to negotiate rules, laws and institutions to open access to equal-status inter-relationships with the world (as themselves, as opposed to as representatives of their kidnappers), and to address their community's distinct needs in a negotiated manner that reflected their officially recognized distinct historical experiences/expectations, and subjective and objective recognized identity and international personality.* Instead, the indigenous peoples would have their "reservations" and of course, the African Americans would have the "Emancipation Proclamation"! Yes! The problem of domestic colonialism is on ice, preparing to flower into a great future global problematic. Domestic colonialism was simply wrong, and there may not, God willing, be any way short of exercise of the right to self-determination, to make it right.

In relation to "domestic colonialism", it seems that some of the European colonial powers—like France—began to understand the advantage of the American concept of domestic colonialism, but decided that the concept did not work well for them. (Note France and the Algeria problematic.) They seem to feel that domestic imperialism could work only under special conditions (as before mentioned) similar to those in the new world (the Americas).[15] Today it may be understood that for the great majority of people in the world, enjoyment of the "American Century" will never begin. For them, it is rather, "The Past IS the Future". The US tried simply to replace the concept of international colonization with the concept of domestic colonization, to do the same old thing better in a new way. *While we can sympathize with the Jewish response to the Holocaust, we must recognise that their experiment to colonize the Palestinians in a period of democracy and human rights is a textbook example of a back-to-the-future effort mimicking the model of the Anglo-American empire.* As one of my bright university students suggested: when we look at attempting to civilize other peoples using the US method, it suggests that they must first be enslaved. This of course is a double-negative proposition. The problematic of how to enslave humans, and the problematic of how to advance civilization are contradictory and lead in different directions.

Analysis of Hajji Malik Al-Shabazz' speeches would, we believe, probably suggest he believed that the African Americans have always been struggling between two ideologies or concepts: one concerns self-determination (called "nationalist"), and the other which was called integration (which in actuality meant forced assimilation leading to ethnocide, domestic or parasitic colonialism).[16] The integrationist/

forced assimilationists were seen by Hajji Malik Al-Shabazz as being very dear to the hearts of the African American traditional leadership of the so-called Christian or Afro-Christian Church, which he often associated with what he called House Negroes—for Hajji Malik Al -Shabazz believed that forced assimilationists consisted of those who believed that forced assimilation and cooperation with the Anglo-American ruling elites would be the solution. Instead, Hajji Malik felt it would mean a final defeat for the potential of African American collective development and their resistance to domestic colonialism and attempted enslavement—and was a cowardly thing to do.

What seems to be needed is some way to provide the African American community with the empowerment and resources, and a road map that would permit them to develop into an equal status *integrated part* of the US (but *not assimilated*) or *to achieve political independence or some form of political authority inside the US or outside. He probably founded the OAAU with the collaboration of the Muslim Mosque for this purpose. The final decision for Hajji Malik had to be reached by the African Americans themselves,* once they had established a political mechanism for that purpose.

Since the assassination of Hajji Malik Al-Shabazz, the UN General Assembly seems to have provided such an international mechanism for such a purpose; it is called the UN Development Assistance Framework (UNDAF).[17] If implemented correctly, it would provide for all of Hajji Malik Al-Shabazz' human rights orientation to be given honest and meaningful legal and political consideration by the UN itself,[18] and for the politico-legal struggle of the African American peoples to go on from there.

Today most African Americans, for various reasons, feel that they need recognition as a national minority for the purpose of international legal protection, and the right to self-identify and to self-determine their future (see Appendix B).[19] In fact, African Americans have already begun the process of attempting to achieve these rights (see Appendix C).[20] Judging from his presentations to members of his organization, the OAAU, Hajji Malik would very likely have agreed with the UNDAF as a first step in the right direction. It would make the political struggle more popularly understood, but political struggle would be necessary.

Although they have a non-Anglo-American culture due to having different historical circumstances, and as a result, have a different orientation to their history, African Americans have as much at stake in the future of the territory of the US as everyone else. Thus Hajji Malik Al-Shabazz felt that a small group of puppet leaders enjoying the assistance of the Anglo-American elites, should be prevented from being recognized by government as African American political leaders. Hajji Malik believed that they may be puppet leaders or House Negroes, whom both he and his movement felt would abandon the wishes of the African American community, if they felt that these African American wishes were not in line with those of the Anglo-American ruling elites. Their loyalty is with the dominant elites and against the developmental potential of African Americans. In this sense, they are corrupt to the core. When Hajji Malik spoke about the House Negro leadership (a part of the structure of domestic colonialism and imperialism), he simply employed a vernacular way of speaking to alert African American audiences to puppet leadership and puppet leaders (a part of the structures of domestic colonialism, and imperialism). This issue was extensively dealt with during the early days of the NOI in *Muhammad Speaks*.[21] Both he and The Honorable Elijah Muhammad felt, without a doubt, that this type of leadership should be politically eliminated.[22]

Stagnation in the American Melting Pot

Due to the problematic of having to excuse the occurrence of attempted enslavement and genocide in the US democracy, where the cultural history and even the humanness of the others was ignored, the historical ways of Anglo-American thinking about the others had to be fixed into the primary themes of United States history in ways that would assure that they were transmitted into all possible futures in order to assure that the non-equal status relationship between African Americans, indigenous peoples and the Anglo-American elites would never be altered, regardless of their incorrectness. In short, there was a refusal to see the multitude of events related to the attempted enslavement of African Americans in the 17th and 18th centuries from any perspective other than that of *the Anglo-Americans of that period*, and a determination to project that foundational 17th-18th century orientation into the indefinite future in American historiography.

Thus both present and future scholars and historians have a duty first to make sure that historical facts are correct, but equally important—that incorrect facts or 18th century orientations are not used as the basis for a present day analysis. The reluctance or failure of 21st century US scholars to abandon the orientation and terminology embedded in the historical record in the 18th century by Anglo-American colonists limits the scope of their work as it relates to African Americans and other national minorities.

The American melting pot lacks dynamism due to the political limitations of scholars who are expected to believe in and promote the "American way". The pot's contents became hardwired and then spread to other areas and aspects of the Anglo-American empire, resulting in a stagnant socio-political American bowl of soup. Each new understanding going in must first be bent or reconstructed so as to fit the themes of the original soup regardless, so inevitably whatever results can only be another flavor of the same American soup. A false problematic of this American melting pot (or attempt to create a new nation) is that they (the Anglo-American ruling class) are viewing their civilization as if it were the pinnacle of democracy, and therefore all democratic learning comes from/through their own Anglo-American civilization. But in actuality, this means that they can learn only from themselves.

Part of the reason for this is that the United States is a state seeking to create its own nation (an Anglo-Americanized "American" nation). It started out with a limited array of imagined conceptual and patriotic political themes (the American way). Then, in its historical development, it required these themes to be injected into all future stages of US socio-political development. Unless a group of immigrants or forced immigrants had positively and successfully impacted on American society in the past, its capacity to improve its relative status in relation to the Anglo-American ruling class and its allies would be difficult, if not impossible. *Each patriotic theme in its appropriate historical framework has to be appropriately integrated into the present and future dialogue. If there were to be a correction of the original patriotic theme, this would lead the dominant group to assert that it was "not American" (because it was not Anglo-American, and possibly contrary to Anglo-American values, etc).*

For example, let's take the theme of plantation enslavement which evolved during the formation of American civilization. It is always associated with the attempt to enslave African Americans or the African in general. The African was usually pictured as being happy with his lot (for all future generations). This was maintained although it was manifestly wrong and politically incorrect. The African is presented as having been somewhat less than a human being with no human rights. As a matter of fact, if we accept any nonpolitical definition of slave, the Africans were kidnapped and never accepted enslavement. If the earlier historians were subjective and biased at the beginning, present-day historians will very likely continue to be wrong if they merely pass on that same subjective and biased orientation. Is there any historical significance given to the fact that the captured Africans never accepted enslavement? If so and this is not mentioned, should the existing important historical themes and analyses be revamped? Another example, if we find that the deepening effort to enslave the captured Africans was intended to prevent a Haitian-type uprising and the insecurity posed by the constant resistance of the African American Seminole Alliance (led by John Horse), does this then call for a review of the politic and significance of the Emancipation Proclamation in American history?

There are many other hardboiled themes that may cause a misleading orientation concerning the true history of the kidnapped Africans:

a. **Capturing slaves from Africa**. Why not kidnapping human beings (or less generally, Africans) from Africa?
b. **Runaway slave**. This terminology clearly reflects the political perspective of the so-called "master" but certainly not that of the African, who is more likely to view his escape as an act of liberation from kidnappers. Why should the so-called master's perspective be used, today, in discourse on the history of the African-Americans? Why not that of the Africans (or whichever represents the human rights truth of the situation)? Were the Africans seeking simply to return to their homeland, a perspective which is also more appropriate to a 21st century historical understanding of the human nature of humankind?
c. **Emancipation of the slaves**. The notion of emancipation sheds an aura of great moral stature on the emancipator (who was actually the enslaver). But in this purported instance, what has actually happened is that the colonists have not so much done a good deed as undone a bad one, through the legal curtailment of their immoral and illegal practices of kidnapping human beings from Africa for the purpose of enslaving them, or maintaining them in a state of indefinite detention, captivity and torture. The purpose of projecting this historical theme of emancipation needs to be analysed in the modern world to understand its significance in relation to the

achievement of African freedom. Was it just the result of political tactics or was it American propaganda? *Perhaps, rather than focusing on the emancipation proclamation, focus should be on the emancipation* ***apology and redress*** *for the damages done that was missing from the so-called* ***emancipation***.

d. **Slave-driver**. Why not call the Africans who were put in charge of other Africans, working on behalf of the interests of the kidnappers, their henchmen or in Gullah "dey ace bone coon"?

e. **House Negro.** Why not call Africans who were selected and trusted (you can imagine for what reasons) to work in the homes of the kidnappers, African collaborators as well as domestic servants?

f. **Segregated Schools.** Why not call the African American school system a "separate school system" that was also unfortunately forced to be segregated, where the African Americans were provided with both general education as well as that required to promote forced assimilation? Why should the notion of a separate African-American school system be so violently rejected by the Northerners? Is it because it was segregated, or because a separate education system might have led to the realization among the African Americans and government that they also had a culture to protect—a culture which many others, including non-elite Anglo-Americans of the South, may have opted in the future to become a part of. The term "segregated schools" and its negative connotation reflects the language and interpretation of the Northern Anglo-American majority and their usual African-American allies who were on board simply because they felt that the Northern way was the only, if not the best way to end segregation. Many African Americans of the South themselves supported their school system insofar as they understood it to be intended as a "separate but equal" school system. The problem with it, so far as the African Americans were concerned, lay in the fact that when it came to funding and other resources, the Anglo and African American school systems were not in fact equal, with the latter receiving a fraction of the funding compared to the former. When the push was on to actually desegregate the South as it related to bus systems, movie theatres, restaurants, and so on, the separate school systems were also billed as segregated, and accordingly were also swept away. Education was an important need for the African Americans in a society that had ignored not only their culture but their humanity (as well as their national minority status for the purpose of international protection), and continued to refer to them as having descended from "slaves". Therefore, in accepting the dismantlement of the separate educational school system along with that of segregation, the African Americans may have thrown away the baby with the bathwater. It may have been better to have opted for an integrated separate but equal school system (similar to what was attempted by the generally unfunded so-called African-American (Black) colleges and universities).

g. **Intellectual inferiority of the slave**. Why not the difficulty Africans faced to succeed in a system and method of education delivered in a radically different language and designed by Anglo-Americans for the purposes of both instilling western education and forcing assimilation. This problematic also occurred in relation to indigenous Canadians who were forced into now defunct residential schools, Anglo-Canadians themselves in relation to the effort of the French Canadians to force Anglo children to assimilate into French-speaking Quebec, the English minorities in the Swedish education system, the Latinos in the American educational system, etc. During a teaching session at St. Laurent College in Quebec City, several of the parents of children who were in the teacher's class (Anglo-Canadians) expressed their concern about their children having an African instructor. They would say that when they were in certain African countries, their children had difficulties in learning in those African schools, which by this stage were no longer using methods designed by Africans to teach only Africans.

As a matter of fact, it was African Americans themselves who taught the African-Americans to speak English. They were taught by people who did not originally speak (and hence did not know how to speak) English. They naturally Africanized the learning process, using African words with English meanings and English words with African meanings. The same occurred with French in the West Indies, and Spanish and Portuguese in Brazil and Latin America: what the non-dominant peoples understood or the way they spoke was not necessarily the same as that of the dominant native speakers of those languages. Thus to communicate with the Africans, they too had to learn how to Africanize their language (similar to many southerners in the US) so as to facilitate communication.

One Nation, One State, Two Parties Fits All

Obviously an African American elected to a government position can only be a true democratic representative of the political platform of the party and governmental system that elected him or her. *In short, he cannot be elected by a majority Anglo-American-agenda-controlled party (with its attendant constitutional and value orientation) to become a representative of the African-American national minority when that party does not seek to integrate an African American agenda into a government-recognized decision making process. Also, the representative of African Americans must be elected by African Americans and recognized as such by the government.* If democratic representation does not entail using representation to address one's interests and needs, then democratic participation means little more than just being there.

Political parties not only aggregate the needs in common among the various groups in multinational societies, but must also recognize and aggregate the unique common needs of each nation (minorities and majority) to achieve the general will. Good governance should not mean dealing with members of the majority ethny as if they always represented the general will of the majority, while dealing with persons belonging to a national minority only as individuals within that majority—i.e. without recognition of the minority's unique developmental needs and its ability to put same into the government decision making processes. If governance does this, the national minority nation will have no democratic mechanism or process for addressing its unique needs, particularly as it relates to the right to self-define and to self-determine, etc. Without a recognized political mechanism for the national minority to do this, it remains only an "off-stage" political factor.

It is only by presenting its needs to the state as an on-stage factor that a national minority can say that the state has failed to respond, and that therefore the state has failed to carry out its moral and legal responsibilities to provide for the human rights protection of the national minority. But what if the national minority has been prevented by the state from developing a recognized political mechanism whereby the national minority was able to speak for itself, i.e. from having a democratically empowered mechanism to speak for it? *The question is: how should the national minority create democratic institutions and mechanisms which will not only allow for the unique issues of national minorities to become more than ignored off-stage factors,* but will also present realistic alternative developmental issues for the benefit of both the majority, minority and the state? Can the democratic general will in the US be so developed as to represent the unique needs of both the national minority and the majority? Simply ignoring the unique (different) needs of African Americans, or defining them in line with the unique needs of the majority Democratic or Republican political party and accepting that African American needs should be ignored (for whatever reason) if they are not in line with the Anglo-American elites, is a form of collaboration with the oppression.

Is the two-party system in the US designed so that it will always articulate what is politically acceptable to the general will of the Anglo-American majority and subjugate the obvious needs and demands of the minorities into political insignificance as it relates to practical implementation? If so, the two-party system in the US acts to force the assimilation of all national minority group interests under the socio-political and economic control of the general will of the majority Anglo-American ruling elites. *This would mean that the many African American politicians functioning in this system would relate to the African American community on stage by reminding the African American community that they themselves are also "black"* (so vote for them), even though their entire program may be constitutionally orientated or created, controlled and supervised by the Anglo-American elites. In this case, the role of African American politicians seems essentially to be the transfer of Anglo-American political will, educational and life-style values and concepts to the African American community and *to get the African American people to vote, that is, to participate in their own forced assimilation, purely for the sake of participation, so as to legitimize the democratic decision making process—and of course to provide (black) political jobs for the faithful.*

The US two-party system never brought the African Americans (as a national minority) into the real US democratic decision making process. The US two-party mechanism seems politically designed to allow the Anglo-American elites to ultimately hold the majority of votes where the question of founding orientation and constitution counts. *The democratic concept of legitimizing a democratic voting process among African Americans themselves for the purpose of allowing them to select their own African American leadership to be included or negotiated in the democratic decision making has never crossed the minds of thinkers in the western democratic countries, nor has this ever been encouraged by the US government—Why?* Could it be because during the period of segregation in the South, there were no schools open to teach political science to African Americans? This may explain why the African American community may not have come to understand the importance of political analysis for effective participation in democratic decision making processes at this time. African American students were advised to study "government", which was what, for many in the past generation, was passed off as political science.

Only a few voices within the academic African American community have ever attempted any analysis of what is required for the appropriate selection or election of those whom the government habitually (when it suits them) recognizes as so-called African American leaders—or whom the universities select to establish African-American education programs. Why? It is important to pose the question, since there is no recognized mechanism and no history of a mechanism, for raising the issue of the need for political analysis in relation to who is politically responsible for deciding what is needed in an African American Studies program. This is due to the fact that the individual members of the African American national minority were essentially forced immigrants when they arrived in the US and had no right to participation in the US democratic decision making processes over their long elaboration. In this case, is it not the responsibility of government to actually provide them with this opportunity, rather than to exploit the results of its absence? Assuredly the US government is well aware of how to institutionalize ethnic rights as reflected in its verbal efforts at nation (re)building in places such as Iraq. The capacity for such an analysis would have been necessary if the objective were to create a just and fair democratic process incorporating the views and unique needs of the African American national minority into the political and legal decision making process (towards an equal status integration of the national minority).

An equal status decision making process where all parties were fully informed of the possibilities could have opened the way to effective negotiations for the maximum benefit of all stakeholders as opposed to some type of zero-sum power game. But for this to happen, the African Americans would have to have been recognized as a national minority for the purpose of international protection. So as already suggested, integration (or any other freely chosen alternative) did not happen. It was ignored. What happened instead was forced assimilation, a process in which there is no political space or psychic space for negotiation, nothing but the Anglo-American law and the historical, cultural and value orientation of the Anglo-Americans' elite rulers: "Their way or the highway."

According to Hajji Malik Al-Shabazz, their way valued profit above all and power for the sake of profit, all to be secured by domestic or neo-colonialisms, the creation of African American puppet leaders for domestic colonialism and puppet governments for the developing states, the substitution of pragmatism for principle, and regional war at the drop of a hat, etc. Same old, same old.

The Anglo-American elites see to it that any African American viewed as politically desirable assists in the process of forced assimilation—and if not, they are exiled (see the political history of John Horse, Robert Williams, W.E.B. DuBois, and Muhammad Shareef being some notable cases in point, etc.) or assassinated (Hajji Malik Al-Shabazz, Martin Luther King, Jr.) or ignored and persecuted (Marcus Garvey, The Honorable Elijah Muhammad, Cynthia McKinney, Muhammad Ali, etc.).

Occasionally, a popular African American leader like Marcus Garvey, Hajji Malik Al-Shabazz, Martin Luther King, Jr. or The Honorable Elijah Muhammad, etc. will achieve power through popularity and the financial support of the African American masses themselves (despite the fact that all of their tax money is used by the government with none returned to them for their own development). But when that leader dies or is assassinated, having lacked the financial or political support of Anglo-Americans and the tolerance of the US government, no significant popular institution will remain to represent and continue the development that addresses the unique needs and will of the African American community. Even the Nation of Islam, one of the most longstanding of independent, self-supporting popular African American organizations, faced a difficult transition after The Honorable Elijah Muhammad's death. It can only be concluded that these organizations fail because their government effectively manipulated their popular appeal, and that they were deprived of the human and financial resources necessary to meet the challenges of their government. We believe that it is fair to say the masses of the African American people have been misled by following primarily a spiritually-oriented leadership that has had little political awareness. *No one has a human right to mislead a nation or community.*

An important problematic for African-American leadership—we repeat—is the lack of a governmentally-recognized African-American political mechanism that would be authorized to articulate the democratically legitimate needs and general will of the African American people. No such entity has ever been recognized by the government for this purpose, particularly as it would relate to providing African Americans with a legitimate right to vote for their leadership at all levels of the democratic decision-making processes of the state (the United States). They took away not only the drum, but also the African Americans' ability to govern themselves at all levels.

Since the official end of segregation (apartheid), the major religious and political movements in modern African American history (apart from those leading to forced assimilation or so-called integration) have generally been politically ignored by government as well as by both the Democratic and Republican parties, except for political purposes. *Today (note the reaction by the media and political parties to Jeremiah Wright)*[23] *any African American who is selected by the government or the powerful Anglo-American parties speaks or can be projected to speak for the African American community. Politically, therefore, there are many African American politicians, and at the same time, no politically recognized African American leadership. Nonetheless, all those who are black (of African descent), no matter what they are or what they believe, can and often do claim to speak for the African American community. The right to self-identify as well as the right to self-determine is thereby grossly violated. (See Articles 1 and 27 of the International Covenant on Political and Civil Rights).*

The Fallacy of Forced Assimilation

At the outset, let us be reminded that there is nothing illegal or morally wrong with the concept of assimilation itself, *as long as it is a voluntary decision*, and not forced (particularly on a national minority). In such a case, when nations are involved, it may be called integration among nations; it occurs after, for whatever reason, a high degree of acculturation has occurred and both nations decide to continue as one. For example, in England, albeit after wars that established mutual respect, and perhaps a high degree of similar values and preferences, the diverse component peoples (Angles, Jutes, Saxons and Lombards) integrated to form one English nation. Note also that integration led to an English nation, not just to a Saxon nation or a Norman Nation. Obviously this form of integration was well received. At the time that this occurred, we believe that this may have been a successful example of integration. However, it is extremely dangerous when assimilation is forced on another nation. When it is forced (as in the US), it does not permit sufficient negotiation and sharing of similar values, likes and subjective needs.

Even the concept of democracy can serve as a cloak for forced assimilation and exploitation to reduce (over several generations) the victim nation into an evolutionary condition of voluntary enslavement and ethnocide.[24] (While this can be seen through comparative statistical studies, it remains difficult for the national minorities to realize the global significance of all of the negative statistical comparisons that they constantly receive in comparison with the majority nation.)[25]

The policy of the European Union, in relation to its member states, has attempted to create equal and equal status human rights, and educational, political, socio-economic and legal policies in relation to each of its member states. It does not attempt to create institutions and policies which act to inappropriately ignore a minority demand or need, or to force a minority to assimilate into a majority ethny in order to seek or find justice in relation to its own legitimate, unique socio-economic needs or demands.

Obviously the continuous wars that occurred during the process of European development have taught Europeans a new or more democratic approach to socio-economic and politically peaceful diversity. However, while the EU effort is in the right direction, it still may fail principally because as a regional effort, it fails to encompass the relationship, etc. of non-member states with member states, which may prove inimical. This simply suggests that this policy can only be achieved at the UN or international level. The problematic is how international organization can encourage peace and justice within the context of each state's rightful claims for a monopoly of political and military power within the sphere of its jurisdiction (sovereignty).

However, when it is related to its national minorities, this statehood need of a government for a monopoly of internal power depends on the way international human rights law and power is institutionalized, and can reflect two fundamentally different motives. *These motives can be benign or they can be pernicious and hidden, while at the same time appearing to be more humane or politically acceptable.* In relation to national minorities, this can involve either the motive of societal integration to secure and protect the interests of a viable state for all concerned, or the pernicious, hidden motive of genocide (ethnocide), the elimination of the non-dominant group by its assimilation (disappearance by absorption) into the dominant group or a part of the dominant group. The latter motive must be hidden if government is to get away with committing genocide in today's global village.

We can even call it ***democratic genocide:*** the misuse or confusion of concepts of democracy (such as equating the general will with that of the majority ethny rules) for the purpose of achieving genocide.[26] Let's simply say for the record that democratic genocide *consists of placing a vulnerable national minority group or nation under the absolute socio-economic, educational, political, and police or military, etc. control of the elite of a majority hostile nation which, for whatever reason, feels threatened by the national minority's political existence or culture and uses politico-legal means (including political parties), in its effort to eliminate the challenge or threat. It disguises this motive under the democratic philosophy of equal protection of the law—that is, that all will be treated the same (civil rights)—and majority rule, without recognizing the right of the national minority to collective existence (self-determination) or the right of the vulnerable group to law-making powers which facilitate and provide institutions reflecting its right to be different. It permits the misconception of majority rule in democracy to have full force without recognizing the need for a degree of special measures.*[27] We believe even Rousseau would probably reject this setup as representing the general will, but rather view it as becoming not democracy but the terror of the majority, which we will rephrase as it relates to the "breaking-in" period of US history as the "terrorization of the minority".

This cruel and hidden element makes majority (dominant ethny) rule even more like terrorism in a multinational state, because it usually masquerades under the rubric of "uniting one nation for democracy and human rights" while omitting what UNESCO calls the most important human right, without which all the others have no meaning: the right to self-determination.[28] This non-recognition of the right of national minorities to be different and equal indicates a lack of respect for not only their equal status but their existence. The free exercise of this kind of attitude depends on the national minority being vulnerable (like all attempts at enslavement) and confused about the actual intent of state authority in relation to national minorities' human rights.

Thus this type of ethnocide has been most successful in the New World, where peoples and minorities have not yet been educated to recognize the limits of state power as it relates to human rights. In the new world, people were popularly taught that because they were a part of the same state, they were also automatically a part of the same nation. Also in the past, many were politically taught that they were owned by the people of the dominant nation of the state. Remember that in order to get France's recognition for protection from other colonialist empires, Haiti was forced to pay the French for the so-called slaves that they had lost due to Haiti's successful revolution. Of course, this also has much to do with the socio-political and economic racist orientation of the forced and non-forced immigrant populations who settled in the Americas.

If the motive is benign, the state can be expected to bring its socio-cultural and political policies into line with international human rights law, and in accordance with the nature of the political demands negotiated with the national minority itself. The best example of this can be seen in the historical evolution of the French-English socio-political and economic policy over the past few decades in Quebec and Canada, or in the same type of evolutionary socio-political process that takes place among the cantons in Switzerland. Or the velvet divorce between the Czech Republic and Slovakia in the former Czechoslovakia, and the numerous examples from the recent decolonialization process.

The fact is that some ethnies or nations, for reasons unique to the objective and subjective needs for their development (regional or international power relations), cannot be forcefully assimilated or integrated by the stronger nation, or forced into accepting the concept of "one state, one nation", or for some, even one state/many nations. Both objectively and subjectively, these nations feel that justice requires different policies that cannot be negotiated within the context of one state. *In such a situation, the nation involved eventually seeks political independence as their political exercise of their right to self-determination.*[29]

There is a big difference between the concept of one nation and the concept of one multinational state, or that of political independence and minority rights, etc. A state can consist of more than one nation or national minority and can recognize for national minorities either some form of autonomy, integration/assimilation, or political independence. The state itself has to meet the requirements of the UN to become a state. The Treaty of Westphalia, for a multitude of reasons, never really achieved its political ideal—a state for each nation, or the right to an appropriate form of self-determination. These ideals were best achieved in the two UN Covenants, the International Covenant on Civil and Political Rights, and the International Covenant on Economic, Social and Cultural Rights.

This lack of international experience and understanding may have caused one of the mistakes made by the Nation of Islam during the three Million Man Marches on Washington. The NOI seemed unable to distinguish between the state (the United States) and the (internal) nation of the national minority itself (the Nation of Islam of the African American community). *They allowed the US president to get away with saying, at the beginning of the celebration, that the US was composed of only one nation, and that only one nation (and not the NOI or the African Americans or the indigenous US nations) was recognized as existing in the US for the purpose of international protection.*[30]

In short, the NOI did not present a request for the right to self-determination (of any kind); instead, it asked its supporters to return home peacefully and improve their personal moral and socio-economic lives, and perhaps to continue to upgrade their political involvement in the US system of what we have called forced assimilation When the world spotlight was on the Million Man March, they did not dispute the president's interpretation and demand the right to negotiate their human right to self-determination with the government, although they were presented by Dr. Farid Muhammad with IHRAAM's written evidence that many from the UN may have been expecting they might do so. It appears that they were so confused about their concepts of race, minority, country, nation and state that they "missed their own boat" that they had so laboriously worked to build, and gave the impression of accepting further assimilation into the Anglo-American system as it is currently established in the real world. *Even if the US had been ready or willing to negotiate, the NOI made no demand that required negotiation and showed no desire for such negotiations with the government.* In short, they marched and ignored important information provided to them from the UN.[31] The failure of the Nation of Islam during the Million Man March should serve to point out, for all who seek political change, that political knowledge should not be ignored; that the particularist ideology of one small group in the world cannot be projected to represent a politically effective worldview, and that regardless of what they may think about the world, it will be the world's view that is most effective. This worldview that must be understood is not in the hands of the village ram (so-called African American elites). In short, political change requires political analysis to provide a better understanding of what is possible, and political science is "the art of the possible".

The fact is that when it is possible to have many nations in one state, this is best accomplished by the systemic embrace of what is called multinationalism (providing, inter alia, forms of political autonomy); and when it is not possible, as between the Czechs and Slovaks in the former Czechoslovakia, it requires the introduction of a new state (the splitting of Czechoslovakia into two states). These understandings (as mentioned before) are readily available for research. It was the responsibility of the NOI leadership to do this research before taking so many people on a Million Man March, from which many will never return, while others remain permanently discouraged.[32]

When the state's intention or motive is not benign, we will be able to see other obvious socio-political or economic reasons why the majority-dominated state may not wish to find a globally acceptable international legal way to negotiate with the national minority involved. The continued effort to control the natural resources of the indigenous nations may require blocking unwanted international negotiations that would provide native peoples with greater protection and enjoyment of their resources. Conquest itself does not confer the right or remove the problem of how to administer (or how to continue to exploit) or maintain an ongoing conquest of the conquered peoples.

However, if the state's intent is benign, the state will be willing to recognize and cooperate with the full scope of international human rights organizations within the context of international law as it relates to national minority rights to self-determination. Failure to cooperate with international human rights organizations is the most visible sign of a state's intent to commit what we have called forced assimilation or "democratic genocide" for the purpose of exploitation, which is done in a manner that appeals to and utilizes the historical ignorance of the national minority in relation to their human rights, and generally inhibits the freedom to study political science, international law, etc.

The scholars of such states often view international human rights law as being simply a moral concept, to be used for Machiavellian political purposes against what are considered to be enemy states. The US fully recognized the self-determination rights of internal minorities in the former USSR, or in the new Iraq where it sought to introduce an ethnic/religious-based federalism of Kurds, Sunnis and Shi'a after "shock and awe". It has been concerned about the human rights and poverty of workers in China, but not of those in the *maquilladoras* of Mexico or Latin America. What about both the US and Canadian historical policies in relation to the so-called "sui generis" nature of their treaties with the indigenous peoples. Does this mean that Canada and the US still regard the indigenous peoples residing in their states as enemies or aliens? Are they to remain forever as "dependents" under Permanent Trusteeship? Is it possible to recognize the need to negotiate real treaties with indigenous nations collectively (or nation to nation), and yet maintain that this is a matter for domestic resolution only, without resort to international law and the implications of, inter alia, the Declaration on the Rights of Indigenous Peoples?

Another major human rights problematic in forced assimilation is that the state's theoretical assumptions about their national minorities usually do not hold water, and instead often lead to conflict, poor governance, human rights violations, and often conflict. This may be because, although the majority and national minorities are treated the same under the law, this does not lead to equal socio-economic and political opportunities or to equal status development of the national minority with the majority, but instead encourages the legal establishment of socio-economic policies and socio-political institutions that are capable of ignoring and hiding the unique needs of the indigenous peoples and national minorities for equal status development, which then become too emotion-laden and complex to fix (by the state, alone).

At this point, the problematic becomes a matter of both the objective facts of the situation, and the subjective perspectives of the parties (anger, distrust and hate), which can be resolved only by the establishment of trust, clean hands and good will negotiations through the use of the good offices of third parties—if the matter is to be addressed without resort to violence or further socio-political conflict or violence. Lack of good will and trust destroys the ability of the majority and indigenous peoples and nations to relate with each other under what either side considers unjust circumstances.

Ignoring the human right of the national minority to be different makes government efforts to ameliorate the national minority's situation appear instead to be attempts to impose the political will of the majority (the majority's preferences) on that of the national minority. In fact, it is the delegitimization of the will and unique self-interest of the national minority that is the cause of unending economic and socio-political conflict and disunity in such multinational states.

The controlling elites of the majority simply assume that once the national minority has come to accept the unique values of the majority, their own unique will and unique self-interest will be achieved, and their problems will go away. And if not, the situation is usually conceptually structured so that it is only the minority who will suffer most for having a unique will and unique self-interest for survival that requires negotiation instead of majority law. If the national minority sees the government as having illegal and malevolent motives, such as preventing the recognition of the international political personality of the national minority (or particular indigenous nation), the conflict is likely to become even greater and more difficult to resolve. Multinational states need viable international legal rules in place in order to avoid these difficult political problematics. National minorities also need the necessary political and politico-psychic space in order to bring their negotiations with their government for their right to self-determination to a peaceful solution.

In relation to the US majority, Anglo-American ruling elites and their usual allies, the existence of 50 internal states (with division of power between the city, state and federal government plus the right to choose whatever state or city one wishes to live in) has up to now, after the US Civil War, served a purpose (self-determination) within the federal-states-cities rights framework for the majority ethnicity and its allies (without it having to be specifically officially recognized). The Mormons, who chose to settle in Utah and virtually control state affairs there, provide a good example of a non-official recognition of self-determination by a minority. But since they enjoy actual state power, they do not need to have this mechanism for their self-determination explicitly recognized as such by the US. Also, doing it this way permits them to cooperate with their Anglo-American allies in keeping these right beyond the cognition of other national minorities who are oppressed.

However for national minorities such as the African Americans, similar to the Dalits in India, there is no such political recognition of their equal-status right to exist as a separate culture or nation(s), no legal jurisdiction or rule-making capacity to accommodate their unique needs. Forced assimilation means that these peoples must find their unrecognized "homeland" within the context of a territorial jurisdiction which is already recognized as part of the "homelands" of the majority ethny or its allies, and is already under the political, socio-economic and cultural jurisdiction of the majority ethny and their allies, who themselves are willingly exercising their most important right to self-determination.

As a result, internal nations like the African American national minority (who are forever complaining about police violations of their civil and human rights) often seek their assumed unique needs for greater autonomy by forming numerous (what the Anglo-American majority elites would deem "strange") organizations within the legal jurisdiction controlled by the majority ethny: the African Methodist Episcopal Church; the Nation of Islam; the Hebrew Israelites; the Moors, etc. These organizations are just a few and are often labeled as Black by the news media. Most maintain a relationship with their African heritage.

Although this process goes on continuously, nothing is done to achieve government recognition and support for the right to develop these organizations. (And needless to say, they are reciprocally ignored by government.) If asked why, their answer would probably be: of course we cannot expect support from the government, we are doing something that they do not want, and we prefer to pay for it without government help. But this is really not the point. The point is that the government receives tax money from the people to use for their development, and therefore has the responsibility to respond. (This is also a legal responsibility.) These popular unrecognized organizations just come, last for a while, and then disintegrate as their leaders die or something else happens. But their ideals and political philosophies always remain, and so become a part of the next effective organization. *These African American efforts to create and develop toward goals that are of interest to themselves and represent their collective will are like the cosmic particles that pop out of dark matter into existence and then pop out of existence and return to the dark matter. Nonetheless, their impetus remains like the dark matter, representing more than 90% of what moves African Americans. We obviously know that they are real expressions of the African American will and determination to survive, but unless they serve a politico-socio-economic interest of the Anglo-American majority ruling classes, they are smothered by the smoke of their political ignorance and uphill lack of finances or psycho-societal space.* Little of political use is gained from their collective development because of their short existence, but much development time, financial and human resources can be lost due to government systemic (mis)management of the African American will to survive within the context of the historical legacy of their ancestors. In a sense we can say that they, like dark matter, cannot be seen, but remain the universal background for African American cultural consciousness, which must break through to define the African orientation to its Renaissance.

Where there are policies of forced assimilation, there is also, for the individual minority members, the exhausting process of having to adjust to the changing subjective enforced socio-cultural norms of a majority *while under threat of economic collapse, police terrorism, and constant fear due to the awareness of being different from the majority,* etc. While both African American and other popular leadership give the impression of seeking what is in actuality some form of political self-determination in relation to the state, their lack of understanding about the politico-legal nature of this task always leads them to confuse forced assimilation with integration; equal opportunity with an occasional demand for special measures (affirmative action) as it exists in international law; and race with nation. These are internationally recognized and understood systemic options; they must be studied and their meanings and implications learned. But the bitter experiences of African Americans have led them not to believe in the authority of books. In the past and even today, books tended to have too much of a political slant against Africans, and were believed to, and indeed did, reflect the outlook of the dominant Anglo-American nation and its allies. Unless this subject can be addressed, it is doubtful that the African American/U.S. educational challenge can be resolved in the framework of a scientific revamping of the historical American thematic within the context of western civilization.

While international human rights law provides for an extensive array of legal and political concepts for the protection of national minorities (see Appendix D) and makes these legal obligations of the state, most of the popular African American leaders of these "pop in and out of existence" organizations are only now beginning to find time to read up on their human rights and human rights law. But they will soon be able to understand the politico-legal processes necessary to achieve them. While the African Americans are still in the process of evaluating the route they wish to take, the Dalits and the indigenous nations have already begun, the latter's efforts reflected in and furthered by the recent Declaration on the Rights of Indigenous Peoples. *In the meantime, the African Americans and other national minorities must demand that the US government sign the Second Optional Protocol to the International Covenant on Civil and Political Rights so that they will be able to bring about a situation where the significance of the ICCPR's Article 27 protection for the human rights of national minorities can be most effectively and efficiently handled by the Human Rights Committee or another tribunal of the UN system, etc. in their regard. Once this is in place, a new phase in African American development will begin in full. The political creation of an African American international personality has already begun with the worldwide recognition of the existence of the African American people as such via the election of Barack Obama as President of the United States. The next step will be African American and worldwide recognition that, in an institutional sense, Barack Obama speaks as the leader of the United States, not as the leader of the African American national minority.*

After the Assassinations of Hajji Malik Al-Shabazz and Martin Luther King, Jr.

Today marks a special stage in African American history, perhaps similar to the period just before the Reconstruction in the South, after the North won the American Civil War. *If this is truly the case, Americans, particularly African Americans, should remember what happened shortly after the Civil War and the Reconstruction ended—the dismantlement of progressive initiatives enforced through the terrorization of the civilian (African American) population by the Red Shirts, Bushwackers and KKK, etc.*[33] Similarly, it could be said that the assassination of Hajji Malik Al-Shabazz may be the event that marks *the end of the older type of popular pop-in/pop-out African American movements and the beginning of a globally conscious popular leadership in contrast to the traditional "wishful thinking" "turn the other cheek" African American forced assimilationist leadership. Hajji Malik Al-Shabazz likely created this movement byrecruiting more globally informed African Americans for the Organization of Afro-American Unity (OAAU). This model was based on that of the Organization of African Unity (OAU), now the African Union (AU). He attempted to recruit political scientists and other scholars, but was assassinated long before he could see the long term fruit of what he had instigated. Both his assassination and that of Martin Luther King, Jr. set off a new African American awakening of what could be an American part of the beginning of an African Renaissance.*

Given the actual chaotic mess that bad policy has placed the US in , is it possible that Hajji Malik could have been a better president for the people of the US today than McCain, Obama, Bush or Clinton?. In relation to the US need for foreign and domestic policy re-evaluation for socio-cultural change, was Hajji Malik not on the right track? While he would not leave us much in relation to the traditional American Dream of the white man's burden, he had, no doubt, his own American dream of a just world, etc., of an America that had the power to assist in the creation of socio-economic and political justice for all peoples: African Americans, indigenous peoples, Dalits, third world peoples, Anglo-Americans, Europeans—all peoples, "by any means necessary", in the best version of "American manifest destiny". (May Allah be pleased with him). And he was just as much an American as Bush—he knew on which side his bread was buttered by Allah, as well as when to stand up and fight (for the right), and when to run (accept defeat created by bad policies and wrongful acts).

Hajji Malik Al-Shabazz' search for justice did not start when he joined or left the Nation of Islam (NOI); it was more likely why he went into the Nation of Islam as well as why he left it, and why he attempted to reconstitute it to meet his dream of righteous political change in America. He accused those who accommodated themselves to accept the US system of administration as it was of being House Negroes—puppet leaders, who were corrupt and did not have the integrity to stand up and fight for what was right. They had, for various selfish reasons, sold out (no matter what they said) to the Anglo-American ruling elites. And for the same reason that leaders from developing nations do (local power and money)—to occupy a place on the middle rungs of the power chain where they could hope to enjoy the relative advantages, creating a type of Christian/Brahmin philosophy that relies, on the one hand, on turning the other cheek when confronted by exploitation in a capitalist/ imperialist system, while on the other hand, holding the elites of such an exploitive system in high esteem, and imitating them. *The primary solution for Hajji Malik Al-Shabazz was to stop the victim from turning the other cheek, and to stop the House Negroes who advocated this as a solution.* Hajji Malik Al-Shabazz rejected the leadership of what he viewed as the pseudo-Christian Church in the African-American community because he felt very strongly that it had been captured by the capitalistic elite rules of the Anglo-American empire for the purpose of teaching submission to their aggressive and discriminatory policies and unjust policy enforcement, including encouragement of forced assimilation. *But in general, he accepted all the religions recognized in the Qur'an and he never saw the brave, heroic action of the Rev. Martin Luther King, Jr. as anything other than the purest Christian resistance to end oppression.*

When Hajji Malik identified a "chosen people" type of ideological development in America as reflected in the notions of the American Century and Manifest Destiny, he rejected these philosophies and associated them with the requirement for prolongation of capitalist exploitation and the wars which that encouraged. The Anglo-Americans and their allies, and eventually the House Negroes themselves, were searching for ideas from any source (Brahminism, etc.) to support their (pseudo) Christian ideas that would mentally block the collective ability of the African Americans and other developing nations to organize to overthrow their kidnappers and capitalist exploiters. On the spiritual side, Hajji Malik identified such philosophies as the work of Satan.

The leadership inspired by Hajji Malik is now returning to the popular scene, and is presently in competition with the resurfacing of the accommodating philosophy of what Hajji Malik called the House Negro. The South American leadership has also been influenced by American popular leaders like Hajji Malik Al-Shabazz, The Honorable Elijah Muhammad, etc., and sometimes they use the African American creo and symbols to describe events and philosophy in the USA foreign policy (for example, Chavez calling Bush "the Devil")[34], etc. *This may indicate the influence of the popular African American spokespersons in critiquing the success or failure of American foreign policies.* The pseudo Christian philosophy of accommodating racism and capitalism put forward the notion that somehow the holders of these ideologies would change their hearts once they realized the harm they were doing. However, this does not jive with the fact that after hundreds of years of exploitation, the African American thirst for freedom still burns brightly.

For Hajji Malik Al-Shabazz, the role of the so-called African-American leadership of his day was not, in principle, much different from that of what he called the slave drivers in the old attempt to enslave African Americans, or from the role of many of the developing world's puppet leadership who have come to believe that American capitalism is the only or personally most lucrative way to develop and run their countries—while in actuality they are running their countries into the ground.[35] Like the so-called slave drivers of old, they have had to kill, torture and lose their own humanity to keep their own countries under the control and influence of the ruling elites of the Anglo-American empire. The globalizing American elites found that they could depend on the most savage, corrupt or ignorant elements of the conquered colonial peoples themselves to do this job, and so they assured that these very types of people (people like Anastasio Somosa of Nicaragua, a former latrine inspector;[36] etc.) found their way into the highest offices of their lands—just as captive Africans had once assisted them in doing this important "breaking in" torture process.

By analyzing the socio-economic and military context that the American governing elites felt was necessary to make the "breaking in"(torture process) effective and efficient, we may see similarities as it relates to the neo-colonialism and imperialism of the Bush and other US administrations' foreign policies, such as the treatment of "enemy combatants" imprisoned at the US prison in Guantanamo, Cuba in an effort to evade any legal jurisdiction, particularly that of US domestic or international law, to say nothing of US treatment of prisoners at Abu Ghraib, Iraq, or Bagram Prison in Afghanistan. Again the emphasis was not just on torture, but also on humiliation, indeed on the victims' nakedness as a necessary factor in the breaking-in process. These historically learned procedures do not exist in a world apart from our own. *These procedures involve the historical legacy of enslavement, a learned and tested military heritage from experiments with the captured Africans.*[37] US president George Bush may have perceived "shock and awe" as a kind of "breaking-in" process at the beginning of the Iraq war.

All the world puppet leadership in Iraq and elsewhere will be remembered for their silence and services, traded off for a better situation than the rest of the oppressed population (whether African, indigenous, Latin American, etc), an occasional reward, and of course US protection against uprising and revenge by the rejecting part of the civilian population. It was the impunity aspect in relation to the UN and the world that may have had the greatest impact on encouraging the vast majority of the world and of the Iraqi communities themselves to remain silent and show false respect, because the apparent cooperation of the world would be enough to convince the average Iraqi citizens that nothing could be done.

As in Iraq, Afghanistan, Somalia and the former South Africa and Vietnam, etc., such leaders who give their first loyalty to the empire's ruling elites cannot, by this logic alone, be expected to seek the best interests of their people, if it is against the best interests of the American ruling elite. As President Bush's arrogant propaganda slogans so often implied (ignoring the logic of "cause and effect") – "They hate us" (because we are better or more successful than they are) so 'bring it on' because there is nothing they can do against us. Or as Bush Senior put it, "What we say goes." These blunt assertions of raw power are more like those of the enslavers and their so-called slave drivers than those of modern statesmen or politicians concerned with human rights, development and peace within the context of a UN-based global system.

Back to the Future

The arrogant logic of the old colonialist world is also reflected in the propaganda notion that the US attack and bombing of civilians in Lebanon is the fault of the government of Lebanon itself for not attacking their own citizens (Hezbollah), or that the attack on Iraq is due to the failure of Iraqis to remove their president, Saddam Hussein—though the only reason either would have for so doing would be to suit the policy seen by the American ruling elite as addressing the security needs of American allies and the US itself.

Given the existing logic of living in a democratic international system of sovereign states, there is clearly more to this arrogance than meets the eye. Similarly, a Bush administration manipulation led the first black US Secretary of State *to tell a bold-faced lie to the UN* concerning the existence of Iraqi WMD. Was the presence of a US official of African descent intended to show solidarity with the third world? Or was it intended to demonstrate to the world's puppets that just as Powell was put in a position where he had to lie and tarnish his reputation forever—for all the world to see—in order to "just get along" with the US ruling elite, so would they...

Considering Bush's historical legacy, this suggests that General Colin Powell and Condoleezza Rice were being elevated to the position of what could be called the global "slave drivers" of the developing world that successive US administrations had wished to subjugate, or in the creo language of Gullah-Geechee African Americans', General Powell became Bush's "ace bone coon". Likewise, due to her willingness to support torture, indefinite detention and killing irrespective of international law and the position of the UN—anything to please the ruling Anglo-American elite—Bush's National Security Advisor, Condoleezza Rice, was called "the bride of Chucky" in certain African American academic circles.[38]

The election of an African American president (similar to the situation which occurred at the regional level during the Reconstruction after the Civil War) appeared to have held out the opportunity to assist the American people to have a real and successful historical Reconstruction for the entire country, one which could permit them to abandon their arrogance of power and racism, and learn from the experience, both for good and for bad, of other peoples: from the African American and European experience as well as that of Cuba, China, etc. To a hopeful world, it seemed it might be possible for the US to use its great power for the benefit of global equal status socio-cultural as well as economic development, and to mend its past misdeeds of oppression. Was it too audacious to think that the US might find a new way to assist the global war on poverty and maldevelopment, etc.? (A true American century)

This would include at least apologizing and then offering redress for the gross violation of human rights of the present and past as it relates to the ancestors of the indigenous peoples, the Hispanic Americans, African Americans, etc., similar to the concern shown for the Jewish and Japanese Americans—not another demonstration of how powerful the US is, and how much it can get away with!

Thus, the fall of the Bush administration was welcomed by most democratic people in the global village. It would seem that, given African Americans' history of gross oppression and violation of their human rights, indeed even their right to be called a human, the election of an African American president should assist the people of the USA and the world in understanding and restoring the relationship between human rights, democracy, good governance, peace, and the concept of equal status relations in America and as it relates to multicultural and multinational states. In short, the world hoped for the beginning of a systemic redefinition of the political and socio-economic meaning of justice within the context of the equal status development of national minorities and less developed countries. For an African American president (given the historical experience of African Americans) not to seriously attach himself to these goals would be a loss not just to the African Americans, but even more, to all the American people and the world.

While hedging our prediction, we wish the new US African American president, Barack Obama, success, and *hope that what we will call the second (federal) reconstruction does not end like the last-first one* (with the massacre of African American federal troops and the people they protected in the South) and that this African American president does not become just a well-placed mirror in which the corrupt and puppet leaders and leadership of the developing world will better see themselves. Both are quite possible because, first, the historical learning heritage of the American collective mind can be conditioned to believe that money and political and military power can be used to resolve the United States' socio-cultural and economic problematic by passing the buck to the poorest and most vulnerable peoples in the international pecking order, which would include many among the African American masses. Mr. President, what if you are confronted with the prospect of ensuring a successful state that has, entrapped within it, a failed nation? Are Americans willing to sacrifice themselves for the equality of the other? Or are the wasps only willing to make sacrifices for the wasps, the African Americans for the African Americans, the Latin Americans for the Latin Americans… the rich for the rich, etc. and really nobody for the poor?)

This cruel American pragmatism works better for the capitalistic interest of the ruling elites than as a model for effective socio-cultural and economic integration and equal status development. This is why anyone, including the president of the US, who actually attempted to protect the vulnerable at an unacceptable cost to the wealthy elite, is automatically smeared as a socialist—or any other label that serves the purpose. Take the issue of medical insurance in the United States. While it is obviously long needed, the fact that the ruling elites are just getting around to its implementation (and doing so in a manner which entails a bonanza for private insurance companies) is a clear sign of the nature of American pragmatism. Different from nations that were not created by immigration, conquest and attempts at enslavement and indigenous exploitation, the rulers of the Anglo-American immigrant nation have a hood-robbin' as opposed to a Robin Hood collective bent. "Ask not what your country can do for you, but ask what you can do for your country." It is not clear, even in the words of John Kennedy, that in his own mind the US cares more about sacrificing for the many in relation to the health care of its citizens, than it does about maintaining the profit motive.

Dear Mr. President, the US is overdue for a societal overhaul. Such a reorientation will further its pursuit of its just place in the future developing global village. Today, it is what we may call a successful military, economic and political empire, but if judged by UN responsibilities of states to their national minorities—it is a state that has failed to create just one nation. It must abandon the notion of building an American one-nation state as mission impossible, and instead embrace the prospect of an American multinational state, at the least. Given the political pragmatism, military and monetary hegemony of the ruling Anglo-American elites, it will not change unless these monopolies are more evenly distributed. There are no sacred values in capitalist political pragmatism except exploitation, eating high on the hog, and greed, etc. for personal profit. The question remains the same today as it did in the past: what type of perhaps soulless nation can we build on the basis of political capitalism, domestic colonialism, forced and willing immigration, indigenous reservations, and overt double standards?

Creating National Minority Puppet Leaders

While we use the term that Hajji Malik Al-Shabazz used (House Negro), we are not only talking about African American collaborators whose families worked as domestic servants in the homes of the colonialist kidnappers. These people, due to their situation and circumstances at this time, were led towards mixing pagan philosophies and religious beliefs that were really neither Christian, pagan or Islamic, etc., but rather were conditioned by the systemic pressure that had led those who adopted them to become collaborators (those who sought peace of mind by cooperation instead of resistance to the attempts to enslave Africans). When Malcolm spoke, he often spoke a type of African American language or creo that assisted the African American masses to understand the importance and significance of what he was saying in ways that the masses had already been experiencing concerning this puppet leadership. This is why he used the words "House Negro". Similarly, in African American creo the word Buckra ("white") generally refers to Anglo-Americans, while "Brother" ("black") generally means African Americans.

Some African Americans who knew little about survival ideology, any more than capitalism, came to believe that if they were of good character according to Anglo-American values, performed their entrusted duties successfully, and became what they called Christian, they would one day become free at last, while the majority always felt that it would take a "hum dingel" political if not violent struggle.[39]

From the speeches of Hajji Malik, it appears that he understood the complexity of the US historical experiment necessary to create this type of so-called African American puppet leadership:

1) Africans were kidnapped from various racial and ethnic nations ignoring their right to return, right to family, right to life, and in general their right to recognition as human beings. The American colonists were so determined to exploit the Africans, or so backward, that it took them years to be willing to admit or to understand that the Africans had languages and culture (which they immediately decided should be ignored for the sake of the dark experiment).
2) The Africans spoke various languages, and had a difficult time to learn how to communicate with each other as well as with those who kidnapped them. (If applied to Europe, it would be like taking poor country mono-ethnic people from various European nations and forcing them to work for an English-speaking bean-picking camp) and in a different sense, this may be what, at that time, the English-speaking new world had to offer to many non-English-speaking immigrants from Europe.
3) The kidnapped Africans had to create a new language to communicate with, under the severe conditions of torture and captivity. Today that language is called Gullah. However, it was completely ignored by government and grossly discouraged by the colonists and their imposed education system.
4) Thus at the beginning of this period there would be

no widespread means to communicate with each other to explain to each other what was happening to them. It is possible that each one may have had a different understanding of what was happening to them. This in itself was no doubt an extreme form of torture.

5) The Africans had a natural desire to escape their captivity, so they tried everything (see *The Invisible War: The African American Anti-Slavery Resistance from the Stono Rebellion through the Seminole Wars* by Dr. Y. Kly)—continuous revolts and alliances with whatever forces or groups that offered the opportunity for an alliance: Native Americans, the Spanish, French, English, etc.
6) The Africans came to realize that they were not being treated as human beings, and the shock—realizing that they were being represented as nonhuman or subhuman—was no doubt an important part of the colonists' propaganda, and in getting the Africans to act in whatever inhumane way or manner the colonists would call human. More than a thousand years after the Prophet (peace be upon him) had preached the equality of all human beings, they themselves were confronted with the problem of letting their humanity be known regardless of the colonists' propaganda. Given the imposed situation and conditions, this was no doubt not easy. They realized that in order to do this, it would be necessary to learn the kidnappers' language, since to them, being human meant being like them. So the Africans created French, English, Spanish and what-have-you African communities throughout the Americas.
7) Most African American popular leaders (like Hajji Malik Al-Shabazz, Marcus Garvey, Bookman, Martin Luther King, Jr., John Horse, Abraham, Toussaint l'Ouverture, etc. were put in jail or assassinated.[40] This was a traditional control mechanism in US politics as it related to African Americans. *The colonists would recognize and reward those who did what they wanted, and kill or punish those who did not. Thus*

in African-American development, a special social phenomenon occurred. Some Africans who had the trust of the American ruling elites, became either defeatist or corrupt, or they collaborated with their kidnappers, having become attached to the profit motive and advantages offered by imitating some of the worst values and practices of the Anglo-American ruling elite—even if it required that they commit the cruelest torture and other crimes against other African Americans or indigenous peoples. They simply forced themselves into believing that being a Christian, like the Anglo-Americans, made it acceptable to attack or be against others who did not accept Christianity. Hajji Malik Al-Shabazz, like Muhammad Ali, rejected this notion and labeled such individuals House Negroes and all other puppet leadership in developing states the same, and as a result, this African American popular leadership was not only persecuted or put down in the US, but also by the ruling puppet elites in most developing countries, including Africa. As a further tool to debilitate the struggles of Africans both in the United States and in Africa, the propaganda was put out by House Negroes that the experience of African Americans in the US had nothing to do with the exemplary nature of the US and was different from struggles in the Third World.

8) The African American struggle had to face the Bushwacker, Red Shirt and KKK terror tactics and cruel brutalization before and after the Reconstruction, as well as the double-cross of the North in failing to deliver arms to the African American federal troops seeking to protect the African American citizens of the South. In addition, African American federal troops were cut off from any of the outside support including, for many reasons, from supply, and as a result were massacred along with the African American (new) citizens that the troops were sent to protect.
9) From the hope and enthusiasm of the first Reconstruction to the Bush Doctrine—surrender or die—turn the

> other cheek became the dominant philosophy of the traditional African American leadership. From this point onward, they were given the Anglo-American ruling elites' marching orders for peaceful, democratic acceptance of forced assimilation for the African-American national minority.

Elijah Muhammad and all the other popular leadership played an off-stage but most important role (ignored by government *like cosmic matter that blinks in and then out of existence)*, by radio whispering in the ears of probably every African American at that time, the time- honored memory, *la ilaha illa Allah,* of the Muslim ancestors of the forced immigrants. However, the Christian or Afro-Christian leadership and their families were rewarded for sacrificing the potential for collective development for the African American national minority. The African American masses were encouraged to suffer in this world in order to inherit the next. African Americans were encouraged to forget their ancestors, and to imitate and if possible to adopt the culture of the Anglo-Americans. Their forced willingness to move away from their ancestors reflected the extent to which the Anglo-Americans' cultural values were anti-African culture. The psychological ramifications of the Afro-Christians' willingness to turn the Biblical concept of "turning the other cheek" into an excuse for accepting humiliation, exploitation, and cruel and inhuman treatment as if it had been sent by God to test their faith, remains a subject deserving research.

By the early 1960s both Hajji Malik and The Honorable Elijah Muhammad had realized that the administrative (House Negro) leadership for African Americans was being selected by the Anglo-American elites on the basis of their being judged according to the Anglo-American value system as "qualified". According to this value system, certainly the more assimilated African Americans would fare better than the others. This is one reason why the Honorable Elijah Muhammad and Hajji Malik referred to this leadership as *the so-called African-American leaders*.

There remains no democratic process for selecting leaders among the African Americans themselves. In a sense, these so-called traditional leaders were literally the"chosen peoples" in relation to the ruling Anglo-Americans. But chosen for what? *For their willingness and capacity to follow the Anglo-American ruling elites' marching orders. This leadership was never, at the time, based on addressing the wellbeing and unique existence and equal status cultural developmental needs of the African American national minority.*

The Role and Purpose of the Puppet Leadership (House Negro)

In any attempted summary of the purpose and role of the so-called African-American leadership, several points should be re-emphasized:

1) The so-called African American leadership puppet praises US democracy (which includes forced assimilation). The African American so-called leaders living in this UN-recognized democratic system do not exercise full democratic rights to lead because they have not been elected by the African Americans for that purpose. But at the same time they achieve their own position as the unofficial leadership of the African American community by their unofficial selection by Anglo-American elites or institutions (Democratic and Republican Parties) oriented to their values and needs. Directly or indirectly, selection as the most "qualified" depends more on the basis of their real degree of Anglo-Americanization. This is true even in cities where African Americans happen to be a majority of the population. This leadership belongs to the Democratic or Republican political parties which were created using Anglo-American values, and which may also be seen as a political mechanism that facilitates direct or indirect dominance by the constitutional, political and cultural values of the Anglo-Americanized majority. This, coupled with their rejection or ignorance of international minority rights and misrepresentation of forced assimilation as integration, as the only form of societal integration, again facilitates the domination of solely Anglo-American norms and values in the socio-economic, political and legal aspects of U.S. society, facilitating the exclusion, as an instance, of Spanish, indigenous or Gullah languages, etc. The so-called African American leadership is blindfolded by the American flag, and sees through their stomachs and pocketbooks. (As a particularly egregious example, the people selected by the state to sit on the Committee for Cultural Protection of one of the most important US African American national minorities, the Gullah-Geechees, have never made

themselves familiar with state responsibility for national minorities, although the US has acceded to the UN Convention concerned (the ICCPR, Article 27.)

2) A political purpose of the so-called African American leadership (House Negro) is to encourage racial concepts of black v. white as a measurement of African American progress and development, even when an increase in the numbers of black office holders, etc., may have no developmental, socio-economic or political significance for the benefit of the development potential of the African-American national minority. On the contrary, it may have a negative effect.

3) This is done to allow African American so-called leaders to place a black stamp on essentially Anglo-American-oriented policy while keeping themselves safe and popular in both the Anglo and African American communities (by blurring African American recognition of the political differences between the unique interests and unique needs of both communities—the majority Anglo-American elites and those of the national minority). In fact, the concept of black v. white may be the sole nod that the House Negro pays in official acknowledgement and recognition of the unique needs and interests of the African American community. In short, *it only enables "getting' dey butt in"*—without having to come forward with any self-respecting plan for government political recognition and funding for the development of unique African American community interests. This spotlights the role of the House Negroes and their ability to find employment by selling to the Anglo and Afro ruling elites the notion of their own utility as subgroup powerbrokers who can deliver the vote and legitimize the US democratic process through getting the participation of the African American community *big time*, in terms of compliance with the majority agenda (the Anglo-American elites' marching orders).

4) The puppet African American leadership believes in the use of the racist concept of black and white, and sees it as an ideal cover for their own personal advancement purporting to represent the interests of the community even as they promote forced assimilation (so-called integration)—even as they and the Anglo-American elites have the same program for African

Americans. If this program were to be recognized for what it is—forced assimilation, voluntary ethnocide rather than so-called integration—it would be protested as such by the African American community, and could be called to the attention of the International Criminal Court, where the puppet leadership support for such Anglo-American elites' policies could be seen as a crime against humanity).[41] The House Negro's racial approach to politics is partly caused by the fact that this is the only way U.S. society permits him personally to survive as a politician, and appear to succeed in the politico-legal environment of the American state.

5) The House Negro is aware of the concept of "divide and rule" as it was used by the colonial powers to conquer third world countries, but has ignored the resultant requirement for divide and rule as it relates to separation of the rice from the husks of peoples who have been subjected to attempted enslavement, and who must revolutionize their leadership (like Mao in China, Mandela in South Africa, Elijah Muhammad, Hajji Malik Al-Shabazz, John Horse in the US, and Toussaint l'Ouverture in Haiti, etc.) in order to address the problematic of those of their own people who would oppress them with the support of the outside enemy.

There are obvious examples from everywhere equal status struggles took place in the past and are underway today, in the modern world. Today people being oppressed must also divide in struggle in order to achieve the desired political unity that they seek, rather than accept the undesirable unity that has been imposed. *For African Americans this means "black on black as well as black on non-black political struggle" for a new, more effective African American leadership, in order to achieve a political unity that seeks to liberate them from their oppression. What is absolutely not needed is voting for a puppet leadership simply because they are black.* A real meaning of Black, like that of African American, must one day be found in the political and cultural transformation and socio-political dialogue of the forced immigrants to the US, themselves. It must become a subjective as well as objective reality. Self-identification is a part of the right to self-definc. It is a process that most nations that wish to be free must undertake.

6) *The African American puppet leadership refuses to admit that they are holding the oppressor on their back while standing on the back of their community*, as in the illustration of the three men (an iconic analysis), two of whom are on the back of the one below. The one on the bottom (representing the African American community) can only use the natural reach of his arms to try to remove this burden of oppression. As in all cases of puppet leadership, the puppet leadership keeps pointing to the person on top as the person to blame, but the length of the community's arms are not naturally long enough to reach the oppressor on top, who is being kept out of reach on the shoulders of the puppet leadership. The community must politically remove the puppet leadership so that the oppressor will also fall down to earth. The puppet leadership stands as a buffer between the African American community and the Anglo-American oppressors so as to protect the Anglo-American ruling elite from the reach of what the House Negro would define as the ignorant African American masses (community). Note: in this illustration the African American community is educated by the puppet leadership to strike only at the oppressor (the "white man") rather than try to throw the oppressor off itself, but no matter how the community tries, its arms are not long enough to reach the Buckra sittng astride the shoulders of the House Negro. So he (the African American community) may give up—*unless he comes to understand that he need only reach just above his head and remove the House Negro from his shoulders, and the oppressor (and oppressors) will automatically fall.*[42] The question is: who is stopping the African American community (with the help of the oppressor) from having free elections to choose an official government-recognized African American leadership? From attempting to secure reparations for the holocaust inflicted on the African American ancestors? Etc., etc. *Only in political struggle will the House Negroes be made to show themselves, because they will demonstrate that they, too, are not willing to recognize African Americans' universal human rights, particularly to self-define and self-determine, and like in South Africa, they will be marshaled by the Anglo-American elite rulers to come forth with their true message.*

7) The intellectual output of the House Negroes is permanently blinded by the US flag placed over their eyes, not because they are patriotic but because they feel that it is their role as "qualified" people to see no other option for African Americans' development than what may be only in the interest of the oppressor. Some may feel that they belong to the oppressor, like his chair or a piece of wood. So they will promote forced assimilation as integration—at any cost to the national minority. The use of their minds is always and forever limited by the need to uphold the myths generated by the US ruling elites which serve as US "historical traditions" (from the Underground Railroad[43] to the Emancipation Proclamation) which in turn encompass and circumscribe all future alternative analyses. *If the essence of all of the puppet leadership writings and political analyses of US traditions and socio-political reality could be summarized in two sentences, it would state, essentially: "The US has, because of ignorance, done some bad things, but it is the best society, and it is moving toward a bright or democratic future So why can't we all just get along?"*

When the African American masses of the US South were demanding economic educational equal status with the Anglo-Americans and their educational institutions, as well as an end to segregation, Supreme Court Justice Thurgood Marshall (now entrenched by the ruling elite as one of African Americans' historic leaders) was brought in from the North (where the so-called integrated school system may have been even worse, in relation to African American educational needs and opportunities, than in the South).[44] He then accepted the advice of the Supreme Court, and led the African Americans to understand and believe that they had no civil or human right as a national minority to a separate but truly equally-funded school system for their children, and that the only way to get access to schools equally funded from the state would be to integrate (forced assimilation). The so-called leaders of the African American community wanted and needed both equal-status funding from the state as well as integration, not segregation. Justice Marshall accepted the Supreme Court advice which in essence meant that integration (meaning forced assimilation) was the only way to deal with the issue of funding inequality by the state concerning the African American educational institutions compared to those of the Anglo-Americans. The so-called integration he got was carried out by the Anglo-Americans in such a manner as to bring about the loss of whatever little control African Americans had enjoyed over their education system and the numerous jobs it provided their community. In other words, they were forced to surrender control over their school system in order to avoid an *officially segregated* one. The question of the human right of the national minority to have an integrated equal status school system for African Americans and all others (i.e. a school system under a degree of African American control, which would be open to both African Americans and any others who wished to attend—a positive acceptance of African American cultural development and integrated equal status with that of Anglo-American cultural development)—was never considered by Justice Marshall. And since the issue of desegregation as a separate issue involved all aspects of separation between the minority and the majority, including every day contact in both the North and South and in many parts of the world in general, the so-called African American leadership felt that they had no choice but to alter their struggle from one of equal status for separate schools (separate but equal) to one of a fight against segregation in general. Thus Justice Marshall did not see the importance of viewing separate public schools and segregation in public facilities, etc. as two separate issues. Marshall did not fight for the possibility of establishing an appropriately non-segregated, independent school system like that of the French and English Canadians in Canada, or indeed, American Catholics. At the time, segregation was unmistakably on the way out, due to US foreign policy concerns related to the criticism that the US was facing in the United Nations over segregation. As noted in the US government's Amicus Curiae brief in support of *Brown vs. Board of Education*:

> During the past six years, the damage to our foreign relations attributable to this source has become progressively greater. The United States is under constant attack

> in the foreign press, over the foreign radio, and in such international bodies as the United Nations because of various practices of discrimination against minority groups in this country. ... The hostile reaction among normally friendly peoples, many of whom are particularly sensitive in regard to the status of non–European races, is growing in alarming proportions. In such countries the view is expressed more and more vocally that the United States is hypocritical in claiming to be the champion of democracy while permitting practices of racial discrimination here in this country. [45]

Knowing which way the wind was blowing, Supreme Court Justice Marshall had given away the educational potential of the African American community for his prominent position on the Bench and "can't we all just get along..."

What was actually gained and what was actually lost? The potential of much-needed separate African-American educational institutions (at least for their children) paid for by the tax money African Americans contribute to the Anglo-American-controlled government, *was lost*; *nothing* was gained. The Anglo-Americans now control the use of all the money from the state and federal governments; the integration exists mainly in the ability to absolutely control the curriculum and job qualification requirements of the educational system, and to decide who gets the jobs therein, etc. Aside from the paycheck to the so-called African-American bourgeoisie and their teaching profession, etc., all is controlled by the will of the majority.

8) *The explanation for this understandable giveaway was simply that African and Anglo Americans would from that day forward just be the same, and just "get along".* However, a truth may be that this Big Stick from the North (Marshall) never bothered to understand the nature of the unique educational needs and demands of the African American children in the South, and most certainly was ignorant of the international law in effect

at this point in US history.[46] His qualifications for analyzing the realities in the South were limited. He was a lawyer, not a political scientist or sociologist, student of southern history, or an economist. He was a lawyer specializing in Anglo-American law, but he was a Big Stick (perhaps a House Negro as Hajji Malik would say) whom everyone was ashamed to question because he was supposed to know the long term socio-cultural and economic significance of what he was doing, and there was no democratic political mechanism in the African American community to officially speak for it, and perhaps to question the timing of his decision.

When looking at his qualifications and flakey analysis, we can now understand that Marshall did not represent either the long or short term interests of the African American community in the South but instead simply accepted the position of the federal US Supreme Court, and accepted whatever the Court said in order to win a victory and thereby maintain his Big Stick status in Anglo and African American communities. Even before the Supreme Court concluded his case, the UN had already condemned the US for its system of segregation but did not condemn the US for the desire of the African American community to have its own school system (integrated and equally funded) (see the US *amicus curiae* brief, *Brown v. Board of Education*).[47]

9) Since those whom Hajji Malik called the House Negroes (probably) believe that any real opposition to the US ruling class is futile, convinced by what they almost instinctively felt was the lesson of the attempted African American enslavement—given its ability to overtly attempt to enslave human beings—that no matter how right or just the challenge to the American ruling elite, it will be defeated, on that basis alone, the Supreme Court advice and decision became both the legal issue and the legal solution. Any other legal option was viewed by this puppet leadership as not worth politico-legal consideration. However, the African American masses continue to demonstrate their will to survive by supporting the Islamic schools of Sister Clara Muhammad established by The Honorable Elijah Muhammad, etc., but without adequate national and international support. Without sufficient funds to pay salaries for competent staff

and all other human resources, this effort faces the prospect of becoming another shot into the dark reaches of cosmic space: a pop-in-and-pop-out-of-existence phenomenon. The Nation of Islam also did not seem to understand that the recovery of some of the African Americans' tax money paid to the US government would be necessary to sustain a competitive school system for white, black and Muslim Americans.

10) Thus after this decision the House Negroes (puppet leaders) along with the bigwigs of the African American community, even celebrated its long-term defeat, in the sense of getting their share of the benefits (booty) that were to be gained by those who cooperated and collaborated with the elites of the Anglo-American empire in making the defeat of challenges to elite domination graceful and democratically peaceful—while the masses of African Americans went on with their support of Sister Clara Muhammad's school system. They probably never knew or discussed anything about the real short and long term issues related to Justice Thurgood Marshall's decision.

11) Recently, the puppet leadership encouraged the acceptance of a half-apology for the kidnapping of Africans and their torture—which ignored any notion of redress and which did not challenge the American ruling elite's determination to continue to hide in plain sight the historical resistance of their African American ancestors, even if it meant reinterpreting the history of the world. The manifest ongoing desire to cover up this defect in the foundation of the US is a good reason to maintain some skepticism about some of the motives for the US domestic and foreign policies. For example, why has the US not accepted the Second Optional Protocol of the International Covenant on Civil and Political Rights, or the Declaration on the Rights of Indigenous Peoples? We should all remember that it was only after the demise of the House Negroes in South Africa that we could hear of the jailed hero, Nelson Mandela. Will it be only after the demise of the African American House Negro that we can receive the Islamic fruits of the dedicated work of Hajji Malik Al-Shabazz?

12) The role of the House Negro was exemplified by the Bush era in power where a puppet leader (Condoleezza Rice) could sing the song,"Glory Be to America", while Bush was demanding

that a portion of the world surrender first and negotiate afterward. Condoleezza Rice appears to have seen nothing wrong with this type of diplomacy, including torture, because given the historical legacy of attempted enslavement, this type of diplomacy was as familiar to her as American apple pie.

13) Bush demonstrated his understanding of the role that could be played by the puppet leadership by getting Big Stick members of the African community (Jamaican Colin Powell) to go before the UN to tell a lie that would facilitate the US invasion and near-destruction of Iraq.

Hajji Malik Al-Shabazz believed that hundreds of years of attempted African American enslavement and indigenous oppression without apology or redress (i.e. with impunity) has had an unspeakable influence on the formation of the US zero/sum double-standards political orientation towards those whom they may see as their enemies (a "send in the Marines" and fire first mentality), and thus forged a somewhat unique US orientation to diplomacy and foreign policy that has a much greater capacity to ignore not only the norms of international humanitarian law but even cost-benefit analysis, leading them to seek to win on every issue and at any cost. *As one Somali prisoner being released from the prison in Guantanamo, Cuba stated: "We were treated like US slaves by the Bush administration, not like prisoners of war. The torture process ignored humanitarian law and we were treated like animals."* Indeed, it was reminiscent of, and perhaps influenced or tolerated by what we believe to have been deemed a successful "breaking-in" period of the US attempted enslavement legacy.

Both the world and the vast majority of the American people were, as before stated, totally disgusted—but were pragmatic and tolerated it because they believed it would work and that the US would get away with it as usual. Until they stood up in support of Mr. Barack Obama, who began his administration by promising to reform health care, to remove American troops from Iraq and to close the prison in Guantanamo, Cuba.

However among Obama's first acts were the removal of the American delegation from the UN-sponsored follow-up to the historic World Conference Against Racism; his refusal to hold Bush and some members of his administration responsible for torture, rendition and other human rights violations; his decision to delay troop withdrawal from Iraq; and his decision to send more troops to Afghanistan, etc.

Were these the best and only ways to go? We believe that most African Americans would say: "If Bush represents Satan—his administration must represent Hell, and Barak Obama would stand no chance of walking through hell with gasoline pants on."

The early decisions accepted by Mr. Obama's administration may suggest disrespect for the human dignity and human rights of the African ancestors of the African American national minority. He seems to display double standards in relation to the Holocaust of the Jewish peoples, giving it due recognition while failing to address the Holocaust of the African American peoples. *Nothing could be more demonstrative of this than the decision to pull out of the World Conference Against Racism at the prompting of American Zionism, despite the overwhelming support for US attendance among African Americans.*

Due to the exigencies of running for office and his awareness of what was required to win the presidential election, he was forced to behave in a manner contrary to the interests and views of the African American community—as, indeed, is the situation of other black contenders for office. The fact that Obama had to distance himself from Reverend Jeremiah Wright is an indication of what all so-called African American leaders have to do in order to be elected. It must have been very difficult for him to ignore the existence of his community in order to satisfy the political requirements for office in the United States. He had to distance himself from the Reverend Jeremiah Wright, whose views are largely reflective of those of the African American community or nation, as if that community's views did not merit expression when they were not reflective of those put forward by the president.[48] But he could have refused to reinforce Anglo-American culture and stereotypes by lecturing Anglo-Americans on multinationalism and multiculturalism. Rather than saying there was "only one nation" in the US, he might have acknowledged what the American people mostly knew: that there was more than one national minority in the U.S., more than one nation, and that all cultures have the right to express their societal understanding. In relation now to his Kenyan ancestral home, in his July 2009 speech to Africans from Ghana,[49] he again seems to have blamed only the Africans for their situation (which has never been an African American tradition), ignoring the colonial regimes and the important negative socio-political after-effects of attempted enslavement implemented by the Europeans and the ongoing interference by the Bretton Woods institutions, and Western states in African countries.

In today's world, colonialism, slavery and torture cannot be justified by any moral or legal reasoning (the *ergo omnes* prohibitions against them in international law are non-derogable) and certainly not for a political reason such as "It would affect peace in the Middle East", or "They were criticizing our ally". But like the old African-American stories about the early African forced immigrants trying to imitate something they did not understand: "He should have said "eyes" but instead he said "thighs".

One thing for sure is that Obama has accepted a very complex and difficult task in attempting to assist the US to rectify the mess that the Bush administration left behind. Just his presence in the White House, along with that of his family, has already improved the image of the American people not only before the world, but for African Americans as well. And this is because the presence of an African American in the White House projects that the values that African Americans as a people have learned—love, compassion, peace, patience and the pursuit of justice—may become influential in global politics, that the proven African American heritage and legacy of freedom fighters is becoming an important influence in US domestic law and foreign policies.

Like Mr. Mandela who, after being released from prison, demonstrated his support for the Palestinian people's cause (because he thought they were right, and he had the integrity not to show disrespect for those who had helped the African cause in South Africa simply because he had achieved power), Mr. Obama (or any other president) should have the integrity to show awareness and respect not only for the past and present friends of the Anglo-Americans, but also for all those who have assisted the African American rights causes regardless of whether they are Cuban, Libyan, Palestinian, etc. Again, we ask him to remember that double standard discrimination, politically or otherwise, is not in the interests of anyone. He should remember that policies are not sacred, and that change of policy can be just as important as maintaining policy. The old African American hymn, "We done got over, don't burn the bridges," might make one think of the new president, but for sure, the African American nation is still on the boat. We cannot eulogize the nonviolent crusade of the late Rev. Martin Luther King, Jr. while sending our armies to kill people in order to get our way. If nonviolence and turning the other cheek were the policy, then being willing to change bad policies and mutually negotiate on an equal status basis would be the solution.

Mr. Obama's remarks in relation to Africa reminds one of the African proverb: "Because of lack of criticism, the elephant's snout grew too long". Not only is double standard discrimination an ergo omnes violation of international human rights law;[50] double standards discrimination against one's own ancestors is probably unique for heads of state in the history of civilizations. It raises the question of political pragmatism vs. honor and morality.

In Guise of Concluding

We can hope that the ruling elites of the Anglo-American empire will see the necessity and benefit of real change through permitting the empowerment of all national minority groups, including African Americans. We can hope that new traditional themes of the US will emerge to create a new African American and American awakening to the inappropriateness and inevitable failure of the ignoble philosophy of the House Negro puppet leadership for development of the African American nation as well as other nations throughout the global village. *Hajji Malik Al-Shabazz would have said: remove the so-called puppet leadership by any means necessary. However, we would say that the security situation today for our multinational state is more serious than in the time of Hajji Malik Al-Shabazz.* Yes, as Malcolm would say, throw these (puppet leader) House Negroes to the wind, let the African American nation develop in an equal status with the Anglo-American nation—integrated or independent. But *let us try not to throw the baby out with the bath water.*)

Hajji Malik Al-Shabazz suggested to the Members of his OAAU that when it came to getting the House Negroes or puppet leadership off their backs, the struggle must be a nonviolent political rejection of this leadership within the context of the rule of law, particularly international human rights law, and that democratic political mechanisms must be established to revamp and replace the role of the puppet leadership.[51]

Different from the conflicts of past centuries which were essentially military, conflicts of today are turning increasingly towards socio-political confrontations using all means and kinds of political instruments within the context of the rule of domestic and international law, democracy, good governance, and human rights, *which suggests that the African American struggle would simply involve having the state obey a political request overwhelmingly supported by its people to accept state responsibility to implement the human rights of the African American national minority. This might mean insisting that the UN first implement a UN Development Assistance Framework (UNDAF[52]) in relation to the human right to develop of the African American national minority in the US.* The result of the UNDAF could be made a legal responsibility of the state with the cooperation of the African-American community or nation.

Before making its conclusion in relation to the developmental needs and rights of the African Americans, the UNDAF would investigate all aspects of the African American minority's cultural, political, economic, and developmental needs (as relates to its human rights by UN standards) and officially recommend appropriate and legal ways for African American development within the context of its US state. The author has been trained in the use of this technique, and has in fact used it for various purposes in relation to indigenous development, and feels that it could be a first step in the transition from forced assimilation to recognition as a national minority for the purposes of international protection.

The Anglo-American-oriented House Negro leadership has not prepared the African American people(s) to create concepts, analyses or institutions that will be needed to protect their equal status with others as human beings, whoever or wherever they may be and no matter what may happen. The political rejection of the House Negro will permit a more normal development of African Americans as well as all other nations in the USA, and create conditions for multinational and multicultural development in both North and South America, along with peaceful, democratic and sustainable development. Our brother Hajji Malik Al-Shabazz is dead, but his good ideas (we pray) will be protected by Allah *subhanahu wa't'Allah*.

This dialogue hopes to awaken the minds of African Americans to rethink or see the potential of their socio-economic power for self-development, particularly as it relates to self-determination: a snake that we see doesn't bite—but even a flea can hurt an elephant.

Endnotes

1 The use of the phrase "Anglo-American Empire" reminds us of the Casablanca Conference, January 14-24, 1949 attended by Prime Minister Winston Churchill, Franklin Delano Roosevelt and Charles de Gaulle as it relates to the war against the Axis powers. See www.ccColumbiaEducators. Also see Richard C. Cook, "The End of the Anglo-American Empire?" Global Research, June 30, 2008 <http://www.globalresearch.ca/index.php?context=va&aid=9473 > and Sohui Lee, "Manifest Empire: Anglo-American rivalry and the shaping of U.S. manifest destiny at <http://www.stanford.edu/~sohui/manifest%20destiny%20condensed%20020205%20final.pdf > As it concerns complexity and collapse of this empire, Niall Ferguson recently ("Empires on the Edge of Chaos", *Foreign Affairs*, March/

April 2010) wrote:

"If empires are complex systems that sooner or later succumb to sudden and catastrophic malfunctions, rather than cycling sedately from Arcadia to Apogee to Armageddon, what are the implications for the United States today? First, debating the stages of decline may be a waste of time—it is a precipitous and unexpected fall that should most concern policymakers and citizens. Second, most imperial falls are associated with fiscal crises. All the above cases were marked by sharp imbalances between revenues and expenditures, as well as difficulties with financing public debt. Alarm bells should therefore be ringing very loudly, indeed, as the United States contemplates a deficit for 2009 of more than $1.4 trillion—about 11.2 percent of GDP, the biggest deficit in 60 years—and another for 2010 that will not be much smaller. Public debt, meanwhile, is set to more than double in the coming decade, from $5.8 trillion in 2008 to $14.3 trillion in 2019. Within the same timeframe, interest payments on that debt are forecast to leap from eight percent of federal revenues to 17 percent. These numbers are bad, but in the realm of political entities, the role of perception is just as crucial, if not more so. In imperial crises, it is not the material underpinnings of power that really matter but expectations about future power. The fiscal numbers cited above cannot erode U.S. strength on their own, but they can work to weaken a long-assumed faith in the United States' ability to weather any crisis. For now, the world still expects the United States to muddle through, eventually confronting its problems when, as Churchill famously said, all the alternatives have been exhausted. Through this lens, past alarms about the deficit seem overblown, and 2080—when the U.S. debt may reach staggering proportions —seems a long way off, leaving plenty of time to plug the fiscal hole. But one day, a seemingly random piece of bad news—perhaps a negative report by a rating agency—will make the headlines during an otherwise quiet news cycle. Suddenly, it will be not just a few policy wonks who worry about the sustainability of U.S. fiscal policy but also the public at large, not to mention investors abroad. It is this shift that is crucial: a complex adaptive system is in big trouble when its component parts lose faith in its viability. Over the last three years, the complex system of the global economy flipped from boom to bust—all because a bunch of Americans started to default on their subprime mortgages, thereby blowing huge holes in the business models of thousands of highly leveraged financial institutions. The next phase of the current crisis may begin when the public begins to reassess the credibility of the monetary and fiscal measures that the Obama administration has taken in response. Neither interest rates at zero nor fiscal stimulus can achieve a sustainable recovery if people in the United States and abroad collectively decide, overnight, that such measures will lead to much higher inflation rates or outright default. As Thomas Sargent, an economist who pioneered the idea of rational expectations, demonstrated more than 20 years ago, such decisions are self-fulfilling: it is not the base supply of money that determines inflation but the velocity of its circulation, which in turn is a function of expectations. In the same way, it is not the debt-to-GDP ratio that determines government solvency but the interest rate that investors demand. Bond yields can shoot up if expectations change about future government solvency, intensifying an already bad fiscal crisis by driving up the cost of interest payments on new debt. Just ask Greece—it happened there at the end of last year, plunging the country into fiscal and political crisis. Finally, a shift in expectations about monetary and fiscal policy could force a reassessment of future U.S. foreign policy. There is a zero-sum game at the heart of the budgetary process: if interest payments consume a rising proportion of tax revenue, military expenditure is the item most likely to be cut because, unlike mandatory entitlements, it is discretionary. A U.S. president who says he will deploy 30,000 additional troops to Afghanistan and then, in 18 months' time, start withdrawing them again already has something of a credibility problem. And what about the United States' other strategic challenges? For the United States' enemies in Iran and Iraq, it must be consoling to know that U.S. fiscal policy today is preprogrammed to reduce the resources available for all overseas military operations in the years ahead."

2 See H.V. Savitch, "Black Cities, White Suburbs: Domestic Colonialism As an Interpretive Idea," *The ANNALS of the American Academy of Political and Social Science*, Vol. 439, No. 1, 118-134 (1978); Ramón A. Gutiérrez "An American Theory of Race," *Du Bois Review: Social Science Research on Race* (2004), 1 : 281-295 Cambridge University Press doi:10.1017/S1742058X04042043,Published online by Cambridge University Press 01 Sep 2004. See also Jeremy Seabrook, "The Metamorphosis of Colonialism," <http://www.postcolonialweb.org/poldiscourse/seabrook1.html>

3 See *Dalit Voice: The Voice of the Persecuted Nationalities Denied Human Rights*, Vol. 28, December 1-15, 2009, No. 23.

4 *Dalit Voice*, October 16-31, 2009.

5 Ibid.

6 See ERRC News, Vol. 6, November 2009, at the European Roma Rights Center <http://www.errc.org>

7 See the International Covenant on Civil and Political Rights, adopted and opened for signature, ratification and accession by the General Assembly Resolution. Entry into Force 23 March 1976 in accordance with Article 49,

Office of the U N High Commissioner for Human Rights <http://www.ohchr.org>

8 See Jan Nederveen Pieterse, *Black on White: Images of Africa and Blacks in Western Popular Culture,* Yale University Press, 1992.

9 Harper's Speech, *Globe and Mail*, August 21, 2009

10 See the website of the National Organization of People of Color Against Suicide, http://www.nopcas.com/stats/, which lists articles and statistics related to Native and African American suicide; see also "Suicide Among Canada's Aboriginal Peoples," SIEC Alert #52, September 2003, < http://www.suicideinfo.ca/csp/assets/alert52.pdf>; and Centre for Suicide Prevention, for Australia, Ernest Hunter, "An Overview of Indigenous Suicide," Springerlink, 1998.

11 See Center on Law and Globalization, "Dealing with Minority Groups: From Assimilation to Extermination" at http://clg.portalxm.com/library/keytext.cfm?keytext_id=163 For a series of articles on the application of forced assimilation policies to a diversity of groups, see <http://www.tumde.com/assimilation-employed-colonization-indigenous.html>

12 See full text of Barack Obama's 'We Are One' speech, Jan. 18, 2009, at <http://latimesblogs.latimes.com/washington/2009/01/obama-text.html>

13 See Karel Vasak and Philip Alston, eds., *The International Dimension of Human Rights*, 2 vols. , Greenwood Press, Westport, Conn, 1982, 755.

14 "The tyranny of the majority" was an expression used to critique Rousseau's general will as possibly leading to a tyranny of the majority.

15 See "France in Algeria, 1930-1962" at <http://countrystudies.us/algeria/18.htm>

16 See Y. N. Kly, *International Law and the Black Minority in the US*, Clarity Press, Atlanta, Inc. 1990.

17 See UN Development Assistance Framework (UNDAF) at < http://www.undg.org/?P=232>

18 Ibid.

19 See opinion survey prepared by Dr. Farid Muhammad and the students of East-West University in Chicago, Appendix B.

20 See Appendix C, Policy Recommendations of the Gullah/Geechee Nation to the Federal, State and Local Governments of the United States in Relation to the Implementation of Policies Required to Recognize and Accommodate the Gullah/Geechee Nation's Decision to Exercise Its Right to Internal Self-Determination

21 See the early issues of *Muhammad Speaks*, available at < http://www.noiwc.org>

22 Ibid.

23 The Reverend Jeremiah Wright had the false assumption that Barack Obama (then candidate for US president) intended to recognize and accept the African-American culture as a legitimate component of the American state. He was ostracized by the then-president who took the majority position that the US was composed of only one nation (see note 12), that of the Anglo-

Americans, which would include their black minority.

24 Such states often attempt to show that no national minorities exist in their state, and that there is no need for national minority protection. Differences are explained as social minorities, like women or poor people seeking their civil rights, as a part of the majority. Of course, this is old hat. The US uses this type of logic automatically as it seeks to lock national minorities into a house without a political key, by saying that they are like all the other citizens, and "free". But at the same time that this is said by states, they find it necessary not to sign any international agreement (such as the Second Optional Protocol) that would give the national minorities that do not exist a key to complain about forced assimilation directly to the UN Human Rights Committee.

25 The American national minority seems to be saying: now that we understand our human rights, you must stand up and fly right, since you lack the authority to ignore the national minorities.

26 We have coined the term "democratic genocide" to suggest the connection between using the concept of democracy to disguise political processes leading to ethnocide, which is in actuality a form of genocide.

27 This approach to democracy simply ignores the human rights expressed in Article 27 as earlier mentioned, and instead of heeding UNESCO's recommendation (as before mentioned), simply ignores it.

28 Ibid.

29 "The International Covenant on Civil and Political Rights and the International Covenant on Economic, Social and Cultural Rights contain a common Article 1(1) proclaiming the right of all peoples to self-determination, by virtue of which they "freely determine their political status and freely pursue their economic, social and cultural development". Furthermore, common Article 1(2) provides that "all peoples may, for their own ends, freely dispose of their natural wealth and resources" and that "in no case may a people be deprived of its own means of subsistence". The right to self-determination in the widest sense is consequently considered to be a precondition for the full enjoyment of civil, cultural, economic, political and social rights. This common Article can also be read in the light of the Declaration on the Granting of Independence to Colonial Countries and Peoples, which was adopted by the U nited Nations General Assembly at the height of the de-colonisation process in 1960 and which equated "the subjection of peoples to alient subjugation, domination and exploitation" to a denial of human rights and a violation of the Charter of the United Nations (operative paragraph 1)." The College of Law of England and Wales, *International Practice: Human Rights Law & Practice*, pp. 51-52.

30 See endnote 19, supra.

31 Ibid.

32 This would refer us to psychological experience with hopelessness and helplessness, which can lead to depression and other psychological diseases.

33 See "The South and Reconstruction", at <http://socyberty.com/history/the-

south-and-reconstruction>

34 "Venezuelan president Hugo Chavez drew some applause when he called President Bush "the Devil" in his speech to the United Nations. ...", CBS News, September 20, 2006, <http://www.cbsnews.com/stories/2006/09/20/world/main2025874.shtml>

35 See Samir Amin, *Maldevelopment: Anatomy of a Global Failure*, United Nations University Press, 1990.

36 For a listing of same, see "Friendly Dictators" by Dennis Bernstein and Laura Sydell, Third World Traveler website at <http://www.thirdworldtraveler.com/US_ThirdWorld/dictators.html>

37 See Observation.

38 As reported to the author by students at Howard University, Washington, DC, particularly Dr. Randy Short.

39 See http://www.malcolmxonline.com.

40 See Y. N. Kly, *The Invisible War: The African American Anti-Slavery Resistance from the Stono Rebellion through the Seminole Wars,* Clarity Press, Inc., Atlanta, 2008.

41 See Article 7 (Crimes Against Humanity) of the Rome Statute of the International Criminal Court, 1998.

" Article 7: Crimes against humanity

1. For the purpose of this Statute, "crime against humanity" means any of the following acts when committed as part of a widespread or systematic attack directed against any civilian population, with knowledge of the attack:

(a) Murder;

(b) Extermination;

(c) Enslavement;

(d) Deportation or forcible transfer of population;

(e) Imprisonment or other severe deprivation of physical liberty in violation of fundamental rules of international law;

(f) Torture;

(g) Rape, sexual slavery, enforced prostitution, forced pregnancy, enforced sterilization, or any other form of sexual violence of comparable gravity;

(h) Persecution against any identifiable group or collectivity on political, racial, national, ethnic, cultural, religious, gender as defined in paragraph 3, or other grounds that are universally recognized as impermissible under international law, in connection with any act referred to in this paragraph or any crime within the jurisdiction of the Court;

(i) Enforced disappearance of persons;

(j) The crime of apartheid;

(k) Other inhumane acts of a similar character intentionally causing great suffering, or serious injury to body or to mental or physical health.

2. For the purpose of paragraph 1:

   (a) "Attack directed against any civilian population" means a course of conduct involving the multiple commission of acts referred to in paragraph 1 against any civilian population, pursuant to or in furtherance of a State or organizational policy to commit such attack;

   (b) "Extermination" includes the intentional infliction of conditions of life, inter alia the deprivation of access to food and medicine, calculated to bring about the destruction of part of a population;

   (c) "Enslavement" means the exercise of any or all of the powers attaching to the right of ownership over a person and includes the exercise of such power in the course of trafficking in persons, in particular women and children;

   (d) "Deportation or forcible transfer of population" means forced displacement of the persons concerned by expulsion or other coercive acts from the area in which they are lawfully present, without grounds permitted under international law;

   (e) "Torture" means the intentional infliction of severe pain or suffering, whether physical or mental, upon a person in the custody or under the control of the accused; except that torture shall not include pain or suffering arising only from, inherent in or incidental to, lawful sanctions;

   (f) "Forced pregnancy" means the unlawful confinement of a woman forcibly made pregnant, with the intent of affecting the ethnic composition of any population or carrying out other grave violations of international law. This definition shall not in any way be interpreted as affecting national laws relating to pregnancy;

   (g) "Persecution" means the intentional and severe deprivation of fundamental rights contrary to international law by reason of the identity of the group or collectivity;

   (h) "The crime of apartheid" means inhumane acts of a character similar to those referred to in paragraph 1, committed in the context of an institutionalized regime of systematic oppression and domination by one racial group over any other racial group or groups and committed with the intention of maintaining that regime;

   (i) "Enforced disappearance of persons" means the arrest, detention or abduction of persons by, or with the authorization, support or acquiescence of, a State or a political organization, followed by a refusal to acknowledge that deprivation of freedom or to give information on the fate or whereabouts of those persons, with the intention of removing them from the protection of the law for a prolonged period of time.

3. For the purpose of this Statute, it is understood that the term "gender" refers

to the two sexes, male and female, within the context of society. The term "gender" does not indicate any meaning different from the above.

42 This illustration, if understood, is in a sense the key to the orientation necessary to putting together an effective liberation movement.

43 While the story of the underground railroad transporting Africans to the North and freedom may be one of America's most celebrated notions concerning African Americans, in point of fact the majority of liberated Africans fled southward to join the black Seminoles in Georgia and Florida, whose encampments served as a bastion of freedom and a focus for struggle against the enslavement efforts of the colonists. See my work, *The Invisible War* Clarity Press, Inc.,Atlanta, 2008.

44 Ibid.

45 See Amicus Curiae Brief of the United States Government in support of Brown vs. Board of Education, <http://www-rohan.sdsu.edu/~jputman/410b/amicusbriefbrownvboard.htm>

46 Ibid. In this case, it is ironic to note that by the use of dolls, children might be getting a negative image of themselves, turned around to provide them with a forced assimilation education program. Was it really concern about them securing an equal status image of themselves and their culture, or simply how best to maintain forced assimilation without segregation/apartheid. As seen in 7 above, apartheid has become a crime against humanity while the same segregation had been accepted but would soon be equated with apartheid.

47 See endnote 45.

48 If we investigate the human rights of national minorities (see, inter alia, Appendix D), we will see that Jeremiah and Committee has the legal right to express its societal orientation. But the wrong concept of one nation, one state, did not jibe with what Jeremiah was saying.

49 For full text of Obama's speech, see http://gachara.wordpress.com/2009/07/11/text-of-president-barack-obamas-speech-to-africa-from-ghana/.

50 Any form of double standards discrimination is against international law. See International Bar Association/The College of Law of England and Wales, *Human Rights and Criminal Procedure.*

51 This was addressed at a meeting of the OAAU, where it was said that this was Malcolm's view.

52 For a full elaboration of the UN Development Assistance Framework, see <http://www.undg.org/?P=232>

APPENDIX A

African American Negative Standing in Indicators Measuring Social Well Being*

• Number of states in 2007 where the white high school student dropout rate exceeded the dropout rate for black high school students: 0
• Number of states in 2007 where the black high school student dropout rate was at least double the dropout rate for white high school students: 21
(*U.S. Department of Education*)

• Percentage of black students entering high school in the United States in 2004 who graduated within four years: 60.3%
• Percentage of white students entering high school in the United States in 2004 who graduated within four years: 80.3%
(*U.S. Department of Education*)

• Percentage of all non-Hispanic whites in 2008 who were not covered by either private or government-sponsored health insurance: 10.4%
• Percentage of all non-Hispanic blacks in 2008 who were not covered by either private or government-sponsored health insurance: 16.0%
(*Centers for Disease Control and Prevention*)

• Percentage of non-Hispanic whites in 2008 who failed to obtain needed medical care due to the cost: 6.0%
• Percentage of non-Hispanic blacks in 2008 who failed to obtain needed medical care due to the cost: 8.3%
(*Centers for Disease Control and Prevention*)

* In each issue, *The Journal of Blacks in Higher Education* collects statistics bearing on the relative positions of blacks and whites in American society. These statistics represent a sampling of the statistics provided, grouped by volume. For access to all volumes, see <http://www.jbhe.com/vital/index.html.>

• Percentage of all American children who are African Americans: 15%
• Percentage of all American children in foster care who are African Americans: 32%
(*U.S. Department of Health and Human Services*)

• Black percentage of all degree earners at private not-for-profit higher educational institutions in 2008: 8.9%
• Black percentage of all degree earners at private for-profit higher educational institutions in 2008: 16.7%
(*U.S. Department of Education*)

• Percentage of white high school graduates in 2005 who took career/technical education courses in business: 39.5%
• Percentage of African-American high school graduates in 2005 who took career/technical education courses in business: 45.7%
(*U.S. Department of Education*)

• Percentage of white high school graduates in 2005 who took career/technical education courses in health-related fields: 8.9%
• Percentage of African-American high school graduates in 2005 who took career/technical education courses in health-related fields: 12.5%
(*U.S. Department of Education*)

• Number of states in which 80 percent or more of all white students graduate from high school in the standard four-year period: 23
• Number of states in which 80 percent or more of all black students graduate from high school in the standard four-year period: 5 — Maine, New Hampshire, Vermont, North Dakota, and Idaho
(*U.S. Department of Education*)[1]

• Percentage of all high school students who graduate on time who are black: 12.1%
• Percentage of all students who drop out of high school in tenth grade who are black: 36.7%
(*U.S. Department of Education*)

• Number of black men enrolled in undergraduate college programs in 2007: 870,000
• Number of black men incarcerated in federal state or local prisons in 2006: 837,000
(*U.S. Census Bureau and Federal Bureau of Prisons*)

• Percentage of all white American households in 2004 who owned stocks or had shares in stock mutual funds: 57%
• Percentage of all African-American households in 2004 who owned stocks or

had shares in stock mutual funds: 23%
(*Federal Reserve Board*)

• Number of white Americans murdered in 2005 for every 100,000 white Americans: 3.7
• Number of African Americans murdered in 2005 for every 100,000 African Americans: 21.1
(*Centers for Disease Control and Prevention*)

• Percentage of all white Americans over the age of 65 who visit the dentist at least once a year: 59.5%
• Percentage of all African Americans over the age of 65 who visit the dentist at least once a year: 40.7%
(*Centers for Disease Control and Prevention*)

• Percentage of white children ages 12 to 17 who have dinner with a parent every day during a typical week: 55.9%
• Percentage of black children ages 12 to 17 who have dinner with a parent every day during a typical week: 52.0%
(*U.S. Census Bureau*)

• Percentage of white children ages 12 to 17 in 2006 who participated in a sport after school or outside of school: 51.0%
• Percentage of black children ages 12 to 17 in 2006 who participated in a sport after school or outside of school: 36.8%
(*U.S. Census Bureau*)

• Percentage of all white students who graduated from high school in 2007 who enrolled in college either full-time or part-time by October of that year: 69.5%
• Percentage of all black students who graduated from high school in 2007 who enrolled in college either full-time or part-time by October of that year: 55.7%
(*U.S. Department of Education*)

• Percentage of all black students who graduated from high school in 1997 who enrolled in college either full-time or part-time by October of that year: 58.5%
• Percentage of all black students who graduated from high school in 2007 who enrolled in college either full-time or part-time by October of that year: 55.7%
(*U.S. Department of Education*)

• Percentage of the entire white population ages 18 to 24 with a high school diploma who were enrolled in higher education in 2007: 47.8%
• Percentage of the entire black population ages 18 to 24 with a high school diploma who were enrolled in higher education in 2007: 40.1%
(*U.S. Department of Education*)

• Black percentage of all graduate school enrollments in 1980: 5.6%
• Black percentage of all graduate school enrollments in 2007: 11.6% (*U.S. Department of Education*)[2]

• Percentage of all American families who own the home where they live: 68.3%
• Percentage of all African-American families who own the home where they live: 46.7% (*U.S. Census Bureau*)

• Percentage of white Americans 12 years or older who are suffering from depression: 4.8%
• Percentage of African Americans 12 years or older who are suffering from depression: 8.0%
(*Centers for Disease Control and Prevention*)

• Number of infant deaths per 1,000 live births to African-American mothers: 13.6
• Number of infant deaths per 1,000 live births to mothers in Cuba: 5.8
(*Centers for Disease Control and Prevention*)

• Percentage of all American households that had difficulty obtaining enough food in 2007: 12.2%
• Percentage of all African-American households that had difficulty obtaining enough food in 2007: 22.2%
(*U.S. Department of Agriculture*)

• Percentage of all white undergraduate students receiving some form of financial aid in 2004: 61.5%
• Percentage of all African-American undergraduate students receiving some form of financial aid in 2004: 75.8%
(*U.S. Department of Education*)

• Percentage of all white students enrolled in higher education in 2006 who were 35 years or older: 15.9%
• Percentage of all black students enrolled in higher education in 2006 who were 35 years or older: 20.8%
(*U.S. Department of Education*)

• Percentage of all white homeowners in the United States in 2007 who spent at least 38 percent of their income on their mortgage payment, property taxes, and homeowner's insurance: 16%
• Percentage of all black homeowners in the United States in 2007 who spent at least 38 percent of their income on their mortgage payment, property taxes, and homeowner's insurance: 25%
(*Associated Press*)

• Black percentage of the total faculty and research staff at all of the nation's degree-granting institutions of higher education in 2005: 5.9%
• Black percentage of the nonprofessional work force at all of the nation's degree-granting institutions of higher education in 2005: 17.2%
(*U.S. Department of Education*)

• Black percentage of all full-time full professors at the nation's colleges and universities in 2005: 3.2%
• Black percentage of all full-time assistant professors at the nation's colleges and universities in 2005: 6.2%
(*U.S. Department of Education*)

• Number of master's degrees awarded to blacks in 1990: 15,336
• Number of master's degrees awarded to blacks in 2006: 58,976
(U.S. Department of Education)[3]

• Percentage of all African-American high school seniors in 1972 who participated in a student government organization: 25.3%
• Percentage of all African-American high school seniors in 2004 who participated in a student government organization: 13.5%
(*U.S. Department of Education*)

• Percentage of white Americans who believe that blacks have an equal chance with whites to secure a good education: 80%
• Percentage of black Americans who believe that blacks have an equal chance with whites to secure a good education: 49%
(*Gallup/USA Today poll*)

• Percentage of white first-year college students in 2004 who participated in community service work: 44.1%
• Percentage of black first-year college students in 2004 who participated in community service work: 32.2%

• Percentage of white students who began college in 2004 who came from families with annual incomes of at least $92,000: 28.7%
• Percentage of African-American students who began college in 2004 who came from families with annual incomes of at least $92,000: 8.8%
(*U.S. Department of Education*)

• Percentage of all white students who started college in 2004 who came from families whose annual income was less than $32,000: 16.1%
• Percentage of all black students who started college in 2004 who came from families whose annual income was less than $32,000: 49.1%
(*U.S. Department of Education*)

• Percentage of white first-year college students in 2004 who had a high-school grade point average between 3.5 and 4.0: 37.9%
• Percentage of black first-year college students in 2004 who had a high-school grade point average between 3.5 and 4.0: 16.0%
(*U.S. Department of Education*)

• Percentage of all white parents in 2007 who reported that their local school provided information on helping their children plan for college: 71%
• Percentage of all African-American parents in 2007 who reported that their local school provided information on helping their children plan for college: 63%
(*U.S. Department of Education*)

• Percentage of all white parents in 2007 who reported that they were "very satisfied" with their children's school: 64%
• Percentage of all black parents in 2007 who reported that they were "very satisfied" with their children's school: 47%
(*U.S. Department of Education*)[4]

• Median earnings in 2006 of a white American aged 25 to 34 who held a bachelor's degree but no higher degree: $45,000
• Median earnings in 2006 of an African American aged 25 to 34 who held a bachelor's degree but no higher degree: $37,000
(*U.S. Department of Education*)

• Percentage of all Major League baseball players in 1995 who were African American: 19.0%
• Percentage of all Major League baseball players today who are African American: 8.2% (*Institute for Diversity and Ethics in Sport, University of Central Florida*)

• Percentage of all whites ages 25 to 29 in 2007 who had completed high school: 93.5%
• Percentage of all African Americans ages 25 to 29 in 2007 who had completed high school: 87.7%
(*U.S. Department of Education*)

• African-American percentage of all students in U.S. public schools in 2006: 15.6%
• African-American percentage of all students in U.S. private schools in 2006: 9.5%
(*U.S. Department of Education*)

• Percentage of black public school students in the United States who attend school where 75 percent or more of all students are members of minority

groups: 50.1%
• Percentage of white public school students in the United States who attend schools where 75 percent or more of all students are members of minority groups: 3.2%
(*U.S. Department of Education*)[5]

• Number of African Americans nationwide in 2004 who earned bachelor's degrees in biochemistry: 67
• Number of African Americans in 2004 who earned bachelor's degrees in biochemistry at the University of Maryland Baltimore County: 22
(*University of Maryland Baltimore County*)

• Percentage of all white children in the United States who are being raised in married-couple families: 75%
• Percentage of all black children in the United States who are being raised in married-couple families: 34%
(*U.S. Census Bureau*)

• Percentage of all white children in the United States who are being raised by their grandparents: 1.4%
• Percentage of all black children in the United States who are being raised by their grandparents: 5.4%
(*U.S. Census Bureau*)

• Percentage of white adults ages 25 to 29 in 2007 who held a bachelor's degree: 35.5%
• Percentage of black adults ages 25 to 29 in 2007 who held a bachelor's degree: 19.5% (*U.S. Department of Education*)

• Number of white full professors at colleges and universities in the United States in 2005: 145,936
• Number of black full professors at U.S. colleges and universities in 2005 who were men: 3,498
• Number of black full professors at U.S. colleges and universities in 2005 who were women: 1,986
(*U.S. Department of Education*)[6]

• Percentage of all white American women who gave birth in 2006 who were unmarried: 26.6%
• Percentage of all African-American women who gave birth in 2006 who were unmarried: 70.7%
(*Centers for Disease Control and Prevention*)

• Percentage of all white American babies who were born in 2006 who were at least three weeks early: 11.7%

• Percentage of all African-American babies who were born in 2006 who were at least three weeks early: 18.4%
(*Centers for Disease Control and Prevention*)

• Percentage of all white babies born in 2006 who were under 51/2 pounds at birth: 7.3%
• Percentage of all African-American babies born in 2006 who were under 51/2 pounds at birth: 14.0%
(*Centers for Disease Control and Prevention*)

• Percentage of all white adults over the age of 25 in the United States in 2007 who had a high school diploma: 89.7%
• Percentage of all African-American adults over the age of 25 in the United States in 2007 who had a high school diploma: 81.3%
(*U.S. Census Bureau*)[7]

ENDNOTES

1 See *The Journal of Blacks in Higher Education*, Issue 65, Autumn 2009. http://www.jbhe.com/vital/index.html.
2 Ibid, Volume 63.
3 Ibid., Volume 62.
4 Ibid., Volume 61.
5 Ibid., Volume 60.
6 Ibid., Volume 59
7 Ibid., Volume 58

APPENDIX B

A National Survey of African American Attitudes regarding the issue of Self-Determination

Dr. Farid I. Muhammad

Introduction

Neither before nor since the well documented 16 January, 1995 report to the U.N. Commission on Human Rights, as filed by the Special Rapporteur (Mr. M. Glele- Ahanhanzo) concerning contemporary forms of racism, racial discrimination, xenophobia, and related intolerance in the U.S.A.; has appropriate research been conducted and adequately nuanced to assess the legitimate human rights concerns and needs of American national minorities. This is particularly true as concerns the unique problems confronted by formerly enslaved ethnic minorities (i.e. African Americans). As is well evidenced by the aforesaid report, gross disparities between the majority ethny and the African-American Community relative to such critical socio-economic indicators as: health, education, housing, employment, political participation, economic development, criminal justice and the application of the death penalty, police violence and incitement to racial hatred are well documented and continue to worsen.

Therefore, within this socio-legal context, the International Human Rights Association of American Minorities (IHRAAM), a NGO in consultative status (roster) with the Economic and Social Council (ECOSOC) of the United Nations (U.N.), conducted a national telephone survey of predominantly African-American citizens. This exploratory and modest survey of 710 subjects, covering 24 major American cities with high concentrations of African Americans, was done in collaboration with student researchers majoring in the

Behavioral & Social Sciences at East-West University in Chicago, Illinois U.S.A.. All data were gathered during the month of May, 1999. The primary purpose of this fledgling study was to help generate much needed basal data relative to assessing African-American citizens' familiarity with human rights provisions as covered under international law, as well as determining their attitude toward the issue of **"Self-Determination"**. Thus, this paper is prepared for those professionals and laypersons, both nationally and internationally, who are concerned about the issues of cultural and socio-economic equal status between dominant groups and national minorities within multinational states.

Except for a pilot phone survey of registered voters in the City of Chicago, Illinois which was conducted by IHRAAM in 1993, comparable data is almost non-existent.

Thus, research which is appropriately tailored to the prevailing socio-legal parameters of international law and the rights of national/ethnic minorities in the Americas, is typically not available to those domestic and international agencies entrusted with the responsibility to oversee human rights issues, especially as they apply to the U.S.A..

This modest exploratory research effort was designed to assist in this important regard.

It was hypothesized that the socio-political attitudes held by African Americans, relative to the issue of "Self-Determination", can be explained by the life experiences of such citizens. There were seven variables explored in relation to such citizen attitudes. They were: voter registration status, gender, level of education, age, social status, race/ethnicity, and geographic region of the country. In short, a systematic national assessment of the attitudes of African-American citizens relative to the issue of "Self-Determination" is deemed vital for any meaningful socio-political and/or economic planning process that is consistent with international law. The following, therefore, is an abbreviated overview of the findings of this unique and timely study.

Methodology & Treatment of Data

The U.S. Bureau of the Census as of 1990 reports that there are in excess of 31 million African Americans who comprise roughly 12.4% of the American population.

Using Census Bureau criteria, twenty-four (24) key American cities were systematically selected as a function of their size (being rated large, midsize, and smaller metropolitan statistical areas SMA's), being part of demographic clusters with high concentrations of African Americans, and being geographically reflective of the varied regions of the U.S.A. where African Americans are also proportionately represented (i.e. east, south, central and western regions). In descending order of their proportional representation of the 710 subjects subsequently identified and selected for this survey, the following are the 24 cities initially selected as the target population area for study: New York City, NY; Chicago, IL; Detroit, MI; Atlanta, GA; Los Angeles,CA; Cleveland, OH; Baton Rouge, LA; Oakland, CA; Jackson, MS; Fayetteville,NC; Richmond,VA; Louisville, KY; Seattle,WA; Florence,SC; Nashville,TN; Las Vegas, NV; Tuscaloosa, AL; Longview,TX; Fort Pierce,FL; Pine Bluff,AR; Atlantic City,NJ; Lawton,TX; Pascagoula,MS; and South Bend,IN.

Using U.S. Census data and computer-accessed listing of residential phone numbers (by zip codes) within each of these targeted communities which had the highest proportions of African-American citizens, all subjects were selected using standard systematic sampling procedures. Subjects were uniformly called and interviewed using a uniform questionnaire consisting of 14 items. Ideally, it was preferred that the ultimate sample size be larger. Resources precluded this possibility. However, there was a high degree of precision and thoroughness in the sampling procedures and data collection process. Subjects' responses to survey items 11-13 inclusive were averaged and generated a composite score. These items dealt with their opinions relative to "Group Rights", creation of a "National Assembly", and the issue of independent control over local institutions and community services. Composite scores ranged from **+3.00 (high self-determination)** to **-3.00 (low self-determination)**. This factor was then statistically analyzed as a function of the seven (7) subject variables noted below (e.g. age, gender, race/ethnicity, etc).

Therefore, given established statistical indicators, it can be safely assumed that the resulting data are highly robust and quite representative of the national opinions of the African-American Community. Univariant and multivariant statistical analyses of the survey data were performed. This treatment of survey data was done to test for possible significant differences and/or correlations between subjects': **voter registration status, gender, level of education, age, social status, race/ethnicity, and geographic region**; and **their general awareness of the socio-legal options afforded by international human rights law and attitudes toward the issue of "Self-**

Determination" for African Americans. Additonally, a regression analysis of the survey data was performed to identify which of the above variable(s), or combination of variables, were best **"predictors"** of citizens' attitudes toward the issue of **"Self-Determination"** of African Americans. Of the 710 surveys completed a total of 686 were deemed of sufficient quality and completeness to be used in the final analysis.

Results

The first 8 items of the 14 item survey asked subjects questions relative to establishing their: residential zip code, native versus immigrant citizenry, voter registration status, gender, level of education, age range, social class status, and racial/ethnic grouping. Of the subjects surveyed 617 (89.94%) were "born in the U.S.A." while 69 (10.06%) born in other countries. A full 621 (90.66%) were "registered to vote" and 64 (9.34%) were not registered voters. Only 268 (39.12%) were male and 417 (60.88%) were female. Since securing a telephone under one's name requires maintaining an adequate credit history, stable employment, typically being the head of that household, etc., it might be inferred that this gender imbalance is reflective of the omnipresent socio-economic pressure disproportionately experienced by many African-American males. Results also revealed that 140 (21.21%) of the subjects had "not completed high school", 226 (34.24%) were "high school graduates", 156 (23.64%) had "some college" training, 61 (9.24%) were "college graduates", and 77 (11.67%) had "post-collegiate study".

Additionally, it was revealed that 32 (4.69%) were between the ages of 18-25, 95 (13.91%) were 26-35 years of age, 178 (26.06%) were in the 36-49 age category, 166 (24.30%) were in the 50-64 age group, and finally 212 (31.04%) were over 65 years of age. It was also found that 517 (76.71%) of all subjects reported living in "blue collar/working class communities", while the remaining 157 (23.29%) claimed to reside in predominantly "white collar/professional class" neighborhoods. It was noted that 519 (76.10%) of those surveyed were African-American , while 73 (10.70%) were European-American, and 90 (13.20%) were of other racial/ethnic backgrounds (e.g. Latino, Asian, and Native-Americans). This 75%+ proportion of African-American subjects tended to be reflective of the average demographic percentage of African Americans residing in targeted "zip code"clusters within the 24 aforementioned cities. The following regional/geographic distribution of subjects was likewise noted.

Region	Number	Percentage of Sample
Eastern States	196	28.57%
Southern States	171	24.93%
Central States	229	33.38%
Western States	90	13.12%
	686	100.00%

Profile of Subjects' Response to Survey Items:

Item # 9: Do you believe that racial inequality exist in American society ?
Yes = 86.57% No = 7.74% Uncertain = 5.69%
If "yes", significant degree = 46.66%
moderate degree = 43.74%
very mild degree = 9.61%

Item # 10: Did you know that the U.N., under international law, provides National and Ethnic Minorities with the right to exercise local control over the institutions, services and taxes of their communities ?
Yes = 26.21% No = 51.83% Uncertain = 21.96%*
* can be assumed that a full **83.79%** (51.83% plus 21.96%) of those surveyed are NOT familiar
African Americans Only: Yes = 26.55% No = 50.97% Uncertain = 22.48%

Item # 11: Do you believe that in certain instances African-American have the right to be treated as a "collective body", and not just as "individuals", in the attempt to address their common problems and needs ? (see Figure 1 & 2)
Yes = 66.81% No = 19.15% Uncertain = 14.04%
African Americans Only: Yes = 68.67% No = 17.99% Uncertain = 13.35%

Item # 12: If presented with the opportunity, should African-American voters participate in an independent election to create a "National Assembly" to help monitor and represent their own collective interests

? (see Figures 1 & 2)
Yes = 60.50% No = 23.35% Uncertain = 16.15%
African Americans Only: Yes = 65.95% No = 19.65% Uncertain = 14.40%

Item # 13: Would you be in favor of African Americans having some degree of independent control over those institutions and services that most directly affect their own communities ? (see Figures 1 & 2)
Yes = 74.82% No = 14.35% Uncertain = 10.83%
African Americans Only: Yes = 81.01% No = 9.69% Uncertain = 9.30%

Item #14: How would you describe your level of satisfaction with the Overall Quality and Direction of African-American Leadership ? (see Figures 1 & 2)
Very Satisfied = 8.52%
Somewhat Satisfied = 47.98%
Somewhat Dissatisfied = 32.74%
Very Dissatisfied = 10.76%

The composite measure of "Self-Determination" (item #'s 11-13 inclusive) revealed that 75.07% of all respondents and 80.16% of African Americans were in the "Support" range of SELF-DETERMINATION for African Americans, while 16.91% of all subjects were "Non-Supportive" and 8.02% were in the range of "Uncertainty". Tests of statistical significance were performed to assess differences between the seven subject variables (e.g. gender, age, race/ethnicity, etc) and their general awareness of the socio-legal options afforded by international law as evidenced by their response to item # 10 above. For example, subjects who were **"not born in the U.S.A.**" were significantly MORE aware of this option by a confidence level of .05. However, they were also significantly LESS supportive of "Community Control" (item # 13) and "Self-Determination" for African Americans than were native-born subjects. This was also evidenced by a confidence level of .05.

Registered Voters v Non-Registered:

Citizens who were not-registered to vote were found to be significantly LESS supportive of the concept of establishing a "National Assembly" and greater "community control" for African Americans than were those who were registered voters. This was noted in their respective responses to items # 12 and # 13. Registered voters responded "yes" to these questions revealing a positive pattern that was consistently and significantly different from "non-registered" subjects. The levels of statistical signifi-cance were .019 and .015 respectively. Finally, in assessing their respective overall measures of "Self-Determination", those respondents who were registered voters were significantly more desirous of "Self-Determination" (at the .003 level), than were subjects who were NOT registered to vote.

Gender Differences:

Female subjects were significantly MORE in favor of "African Americans having some degree of independent control over institutions and services that most directly affect their own community", than were male subjects. This was revealed by way of their respective responses to survey item # 13, and a .009 level of statistical significance. Similarly, female respondents also showed a composite "Self-Determination" score that was significantly more supportive than were their male counterparts (.022 level of confidence).

Social Class Differences:

Those subjects living is "Blue-collar/Working-Class" neighborhoods were significantly more in favor of the independent creation of a "National Assembly" and increased "Community Control" for African Americans than were respondents living in "White-Collar/Professional Class" communities. This was confirmed by their responses to items #'s 12 and 13 , and .000 levels of statistical significance respectively. Similarly, respondents living in "Blue-Collar/ Working- Class" communities expressed a signifi-cantly greater desire for "Self-Determination" than did their "White-Collar/Professional Class" counterparts. This was also evidenced by a .000 confidence level. However, it should be noted that in spite of this variation it is still important to realize that irrespec-tive of the variables of social-class, age, gender, race/ethnicity, education, etc.; **75%** of all citizens and **80%** of African Americans were in the "support" range of expressing "Self-Determination" for African Americans.

Racial/Ethnic Differences:

Data revealed that African-American subjects believed that the **magnitude** of the degree of racial inequality in American society is far greater than that perceived by all the "Non-African-American" subjects combined (item # 9B, .002 level of confidence). "Non-African-American" subjects, as a group, were significantly **far less supportive** of the independent creation of a "National Assembly" for African-American citizens than were African-American citizens themselves. This sharp difference was noted in their respective responses to item # 12, and a .000 level of statistical significance. Also, as a group, all "Non-African-American" respondents differed significantly from the African-American subjects in that the former were **much less supportive** of "African Americans having some degree of independent control over those institutions and services that most directly affect their own communities". This difference was noted in their respective responses to item # 13, and a .000 confidence level. **This was true in spite of the fact that a resounding 81% of all African-American citizens responded "yes" to this item.** Finally, results likewise revealed that "Non-African-American" respondents were also significantly **less** inclined to express support for African-American "Self-Determination" than were African Americans themselves (.000 level of statistical significance noted). Conversely, **African-American citizens** were dramatically **much more in support** of **"Self-Determination"** for African Americans than were European-Americans (difference at .000 level of confidence) or, as mentioned, all other racial/ethnic groups combined.

Educational Differences:

To insure that the possible interaction of the "race/ethnicity", "social class" and "education" variables did not inadvertently give rise to a faulty analysis, the "education" profile of ONLY those respondents who are African-American was used for this assess-ment. Therefore, any statistical variations that might be noted would be attributable to the true differences in "educational" background only. In most instances, results indicated that this variable did not significantly contribute to major differences in the responses of African-American subjects. However, several interesting patterns did emerge. For example, African Americans having completed at least a B.A. degree and those having "Graduate/Professional School" training—as opposed to those with **less than 12 years** of education—were significantly MORE inclined to believe that

"African Americans have the right to be treated as a 'collective body', and not just as 'individuals', in the attempt to address their common problems and concerns". This was noted by their responses to item # 11, and confidence levels of .03 and .04 respectively. Finally, results further indicated that those African Americans having "some college" were significantly **more dissatisfied** with the "overall quality and direction of African-American Leadership" than were those who completed less than the 12th grade. This was confirmed at the .01 level of significance.

Age Differences:

Results indicated that in most instances the "age" variable, on balance, did not significantly contribute to major differences in subjects' responses. However, just one notable pattern was detected. Subjects in the 36-49 year old cohort tended to be significantly more dissatisfied with the "overall quality and direction of today's African-American Leadership" than were citizens in the 65+ year old age bracket (.03 confidence level). No other significant differences were detected.

Geographic/Regional Differences:

The survey revealed that citizens in the Eastern Region of the U.S.A., who agreed that "racial inequality exist in American society", felt that such inequality exists to a more significant degree than do similar subjects who reside in either the Southern or Central Regions of the country. This was evidenced by levels of statistical significance of .017 and .020 respectively. Similarly, subjects from the Western Region of the U.S.A. also differed from subjects in South in this regard (.019 level of confidence) and also from citizens in the Central States (.026 level) , in that they too reported experiencing a **greater degree** of "inequality". Additionally, citizens in the Central Region of the U.S.A. responded with greater favor ability to item # 11 (i.e. the right to be treated as a "collective body") than did subjects in either the Eastern or Southern Regions (.021 and .000 levels respectively). Citizens from the Central States also responded more favorably to the issue of "community control" (item # 13) than did those in the Southern portion of the U.S.A. (.056 level). Lastly, and most importantly, it was noted that citizens in the Eastern Region of the U.S.A. were **stronger supporters** of **"Self-Determination"** for African Americans than those in the South (.049 level), while subjects in the Central States were even **more strongly supportive** than both citizens in the Eastern and Southern Regions of America (confidence levels of .058 and .000 respectively). It should be noted, however, that all regions of the country were well within the overall **75%** national "support range" for "Self-Determination" for African-American citizens. In looking at each of the 24 cities investigated, the data suggests that, in the following order, the cities of Detroit, Michigan; Chicago, Illinois and New York City, New York have voiced the most notable and positive expression of "Self-Determination" for African-American citizens.

Regression Analysis of Data:

The above described univariate (t-test) analyses permitted the detection of any area(s) of statistically significant differences between subject variables (i.e. voter registration status, gender, age, education, race/ethnicity, etc), and their corresponding response pattern to survey items #'s 9 - 14 inclusive. Major differences have been noted and profiled above. However, a more robust and comprehensive regression analysis of the data was likewise performed (see Figure 3). This was done to determine which of the above noted subject variables, singularly and/or in combination, would be the best predictor(s) of a "positive" or "negative" measure of "Self-Determination". Such a regression analysis revealed that the singularly most potent predictor of citizen attitudes in this regard was race/ethnicity (P-value of .000 level of confidence). Additionally, and in descending order, such factors as the subjects' level of education, social class, being "registered v not-registered" to vote; were also found to have significant predictive influence on citizen opinions concerning "Self-Determination". Such influence was noted by P-values of .020,.021, and .031 respectively.

Discussion & Recommendations

The International Human Rights Association of American Minorities (IHRAAM), a NGO in consultative status with the United Nations (U.N.), conducted a national phone survey of 710 systematically sampled and predominantly African-American subjects

during the month of May, 1999. Subjects were selected from 24 key cities throughout the U.S.A., which represented demographically/ geographically stratified cross-sections of those territorial clusters where African-American citizens are predominantly concen-trated as evidenced by U.S. Bureau of Census data. The purpose of this survey was to generate much needed basal information relative to citizen awareness of the socio-legal options afforded by international Human Rights Law, and attitudes regarding the issue of "Self-Determination" for African Americans.

Seven (7) subject variables were explored in relation to citizen awareness and attitude scores. These variables were: voter registration status, gender, level of education, age, social status, race/ethnicity, and geographic region of residence. The systematic sample ultimately resulted in a total of 686 usable surveys. A more detailed profile of subject characteristics are summarized above. While 90% were born in the U.S.A., 10% came from other countries. Ninety-one (91%) were registered to vote while 9% were not. Only 39% were male and 61% were female. It was noted that 21% had "not" completed high school, 34% were high school graduates, 24% had completed "some college", 9% were college graduates, and 12% had some level of "post-collegiate" study. Subject ages ranged from 18-65+ years of age, while 77% reported living in "blue-collar/working class" communities, and 23% claimed to reside in "white-collar/professional class" neighborhoods. It was noted that 76% of the citizens surveyed were African-American, 11% were European-Americans, and 13% were of other racial/ethnic backgrounds.

Finally, results indicated that 29% of the citizens surveyed resided in the Eastern Regions of the U.S.A., 25% in the Southern States, 33% in the Central Region, and 13% in the Western Region. All data compiled were subject to thorough statistical analyses.

Several subject variables were proven to be significantly related to the attitudes expressed regarding "Self-Determination". In short, a regression analysis revealed that the singularly most potent predictor of "positive" citizen attitudes toward this issue was race/ethnicity. It was found that African-American citizens, in aggregate, who have "college level" training, live in "blue-collar/working class" neighborhoods, and who are "registered voters"; demonstrate the statistically **strongest desire** to have their 'collective rights" recognized, create an independent National Assembly to represent their common interests, and to "exert independent control over those institutions and services that most directly affect their own communities". Conversely, "Non-African-American" citizens, as a group, and those who are not "native-born", live in the Southern Region of the U.S.A., and are over 65 years of age; represent those who are statistically far **less supportive** of these goals.

Recommendations:

In light of the results of this exploratory survey, it is respectfully recommended that:

(1) The U.N. Human Rights Commission, along with the Special Working Group on Minorities, and World Conference Against Racism (WCAR),should take special note of the potential implications of these exploratory findings; particularly as relates to the internationally binding obligations of the U.S.A..

(2) In its capacity as a NGO in consultative status (roster) with the Economic & Social Council of the U.N., IHRAAM is both willing and able to collaborate with any/all appropriate local/national/international organizations in the further articulation of any future research and/or cognate activities that might be suggested by this investigation.

(3) It is strongly recommended that similar and more comprehensive investigativestudies relative to the concerns of national/ethnic minorities be conducted throughout the U.S.A. and other appropriate nations in the Americas.

(4) In light of the overwhelming and statistically significant indications that African-American citizens are strongly desirous of exploring options leading to "Self-Determination" of their communities (in accordance with national/international law); it is strongly recommended that formal steps be taken to conduct a "National Plebiscite" on this issue among all African-American voters, while similarly striving to establish a "National Consultative Assembly" which would help monitor and oversee their collective concerns.

APPENDIX C

POLICY RECOMMENDATIONS
OF THE
GULLAH/GEECHEE NATION
TO THE
FEDERAL, STATE AND LOCAL GOVERNMENTS OF THE UNITED STATES*

On behalf of the Gullah/Geechee Council of Elders (Wisdom Circle) and with its Chieftess, it is an honor for us to present our demand for an historic new partnership with the Anglo-Carolinean and other Americans designed to implement the international human right to self-determination as a form of reparations for the enslavement of our African ancestors and consequent segregation and continuing racial oppression of their descendants.

The recognition of the human right to Self-determination of the Gullah/Geechee people is provided for under Article 27 of the International Covenant on Civil and Political Rights.[1] Thus we request that the government of the great state of South Carolina, in cooperation with the Federal Government, make recognition of the right of Gullah/Geechees to self-determination a cornerstone of future government policy..

The development, negotiation and implementation of this new policy should include a broad-based consultation process which will involve the Chieftess and representation from the Council of Elders (Wisdom Circle) at local, regional and national levels, as well as all state and local governments and federal officials who would be involved.

---

* This document, titled in full *Policy Recommendations of the Gullah/Geechee Nation to the Federal, State and Local Governments of the United States in Relation to the Implementation of Policies Required to Recognize and Accommodate the Gullah/ Geechee's Decision to Exercise Its Right to Internal Self-Determination,* was adopted by the Gullah/Geechee's governing Wisdom Council of Elders in 2002. See also UN Commentary on the Declaration on the Rights of Persons Belonging to National or Ethnic Minorities, Appendix D, which was appended to this original document..

The desire of the Gullah to negotiate our institutional relationship with our fellow Americans of is clear: Gullah/Geechee survival demands that significant institutional change must be made to ensure the Gullah/Geechee people have greater control over their communities and lives. Therefore, we believe that the most just, reasonable and practical mechanism to achieve this is through negotiated agreements.

Therefore it is imperative that we as South Carolineans and Americans work towards achieving change in pragmatic and responsible ways. We realize that the challenge to make this a reality rests on the commitment of all parties, Anglo-Carolinians generally, all levels of governments and Gullah/Geechees.

We are proud to present this policy which will mark a fundamental improvement in how the local, state and federal governments will work together with Gullah/ Geechee people in the future, enhancing our co-existence and national solidarity for generations to come.

Chieftess
Circle of Elders (Wisdom Circle)

MOTION

We, the Council of Elders, move that the State of South Carolina now recognize the human right of self-determination of the Gullah/Geechee people as an existing right and develop an approach to implementation that focuses on reaching practical and workable agreements on how self-determination will be exercised, rather than trying to define it in abstract terms. The Council of Elders believes that this approach can be flexible and can allow all interested parties to make an appropriate input into this process in the realization of Gullah/Geechee self-determination.

While significant differences remain among Gullah/Geechee people on the meaning of self-determination, most Gullah/Geechee would agree that it is time to start working together toward making Gullah/Geechee self-determination a means of unleashing their developmental potential.

The goal of the Gullah/Geechee leadership as well as the local, state and federal governments should be to initiate a process that will allow practical progress to be made, to restore dignity to the Gullah/Geechee people and empower them to become self-reliant. Therefore, the Gullah/Geechee people need to be able to exercise structures of governance that can and will govern in a manner that is responsive to the unique needs and interests of the Gullah/Geechee people. Thus we believe that like most other national minorities or nations in multinational states, the Gull ah/Geechee nation or people, in order to achieve equal status development, must be granted the following:

1) Our Orientation: The Most Fundamental Human Right in International Law: The Right to Self-determination

The state and federal governments of the United States, in recognizing the human right of self-determination as an existing Gullah/Geechee right, must recognize that the Gullah/Geechee people, as citizens of the United States, have the right to govern themselves in relation to matters that are internal to their communities, integral to their unique culture, identity, traditions, languages and institutions, and where applicable, with respect to their special relationship to their land and their resources.

The Council of Elders realizes that this human right to self-determination for the Gullah/Geechee people may be enforceable by the courts; that there is and will be differences of views between the government and Gullah/Geechees as well as among the Gullah/Geechees themselves about the nature, scope and content of implementation of this right, and thus litigation over the human right would be lengthy, costly and would tend to foster conflict. Therefore, the Council recommends that the courts' role be limited to providing general guidance to the parties, leaving it to them to work out detailed arrangements through arbitration, mediation and conflict resolution.

Also for these reasons, the Council is convinced that litigation should be a last resort. Negotiations among governments and the Gullah/Geechee people are clearly preferable as the most practical and effective way to implement the human right of self-determination.

The Nature and Scope of Gullah/Geechee Self-determination

The Gullah/Geechee people seek internal self-determination. Gullah/Geechee governments and institutions exercising the human right of self-determination will operate within the framework of the American Constitution. Gullah/Geechee jurisdictions and authorities should, therefore, work in harmony with jurisdictions that are exercised by other governments. It is in the interest of both Gullah/Geechee and non-Gullah/Geechee governments to develop co-operative arrangements that will ensure the harmonious relationship of laws which is indispensable to the proper functioning of the USA as a whole.

In light of the wide array of Gullah/Geechee jurisdictions or authorities that may be the subject of negotiations, state governments should be the most important parties to negotiations and agreements since subject matters being negotiated normally fall within state jurisdiction and where in most subject matters being negotiated will have no impact beyond the state wherein the Gullah/Geechee group in question resides.

It is the choice of the Gullah/Geechee people that their right to self-determination in the international law sense, should not mean a politically independent Gullah/

Geechee state. On the contrary, implementation of self-determination should enhance the participation of the Gullah/Geechee people in the American socio-economic and political system by enlarging the scope of the U.S. institutions to include their special needs and identity, and ensure that the Gullah/Geechee people and their governments do not continue to exist in de facto isolation, separate and apart from equal status development with the rest of the American peoples.

American Bill of Rights and Article 27 of the International Covenant on Civil and Political Rights

The Council is committed to the principle that the American Bill of Rights as well as Article 27 of the International Covenant on Civil and Political Rights should bind all governments in the United States, so that Gullah/Geechees and non-Gullah/Geechee alike may continue to enjoy equally the rights and freedoms guaranteed by these instruments. Self-determination agreements will, therefore, have to provide that the American Bill of Rights and Article 27 of the International Covenant on Civil and Political Rights applies to Gullah/Geechee governments and institutions in relation to all matters within their respective jurisdictions and authorities.

The American Bill of Rights is thus seen by the Gullah/Geechee Council as designed to ensure a sensitive balance between individual rights and freedoms, and the unique values and traditions and collective rights of the Gullah/Geechee peoples in the United States.

Non-Territorial Self-determination

Due to the fact that Gullah/Geechees do not form a majority in any existing U.S. territorial/political entity, Gullah/Geechee self-determination will in most cases be non-territorial. Also, given the vastly different circumstances of Gullah/Geechees throughout the United States, implementation of the human right to self-determination cannot be uniform across the country or result in a "one-size-fits-all" form of self-determination. The Council proposes to negotiate self-determination arrangements that are tailored to meet the unique needs of the Gullah/Geechee people as a whole, while providing for appropriate responses to the particular political, economic, legal, historical, cultural and social circumstances of particular groups and individuals.

Scope of Negotiations

Under the Gullah/Geechee Council of Elders' approach, the central objective of negotiations will be to reach agreements on self-determination as opposed to legal definitions of the human right to self-determination. The Government realizes that Gullah/Geechee governments and institutions will require the jurisdiction or authority to act in a number of societal sectors in order to give practical effect to the human right of self-determination. Broadly stated, the Council of Elders views the scope of Gullah/Geechee jurisdiction or authority as likely extending to matters that are internal to the group, integral to its distinct Gullah/Geechee culture and developmental needs, and essential to the ability of the Gullah/Geechee nation to operate as a third or fourth level government or governing institution. Under this approach, the range of matters that would be raised as subjects for negotiation with the government could include all, some, or parts of the following:

- establishment of governing structures, an internal constitution, elections, leadership selection processes
- membership (citizenship in the Gullah/Geechee nation)
- marriage
- adoption and child welfare
- education
- health
- social services
- administration/enforcement of Gullah/Geechee laws, including the establishment of Gullah/Geechee courts or tribunals and the creation of penalties of the type normally created by local or regional governments for contravention of their laws
- policing
- property rights, including succession and estates
- where appropriate, land management, including: zoning; service fees; land tenure and access; and expropriation of any land that may be negotiated as Gullah/Geechee by Gullah/Geechee governments for their own public purposes
- natural resources management
- taxation in respect of direct taxes and property taxes
- transfer and management of monies and group assets
- management of public works and infrastructure
- housing
- local transportation
- licensing, regulation, and accreditation of societies for professionals such as lawyers, psychologists, etc. intending to work in the Gullah/Geechee communities

In some of these areas, detailed arrangements will be required to ensure harmonization of laws, while in others, a more general recognition of Gullah/Geechee jurisdiction or authority may be sufficient.

There are a number of other areas that may go beyond matters that are integral to Gullah/Geechee culture or that are strictly internal to a Gullah/Geechee group. To the extent that the federal government has jurisdiction in such areas, it should be prepared to negotiate some measure of Gullah/Geechee jurisdiction or authority, because in these areas, laws and regulations will tend to have impacts that go beyond individual Gullah/Geechee communities. Therefore, primary law-making authority would remain with the federal or state governments, as the case may be, and their laws would prevail in the event of a conflict with Gullah/Geechee laws. Subject matters in this category would include:

- divorce
- administration of justice issues, including matters related to the administration and enforcement of laws of other jurisdictions which might include certain criminal laws
- penitentiaries and parole
- environmental protection, assessment and pollution prevention
- emergency preparedness
- etc.

There are a number of subject matters where there may be no compelling reasons for Gullah/Geechee governments or institutions to exercise law-making authority. These subject matters cannot be characterized as either integral to Gullah/Geechee cultures, or internal to Gullah/Geechee community needs. They can be grouped under two headings: (i) powers related to U.S. sovereignty, defence and external relations; and (ii) other national interest powers. In these areas, it is essential that the federal government retain its law-making primacy, with a willingness to negotiate special measures to accommodate Gullah/Geechee interests where appropriate. Subject matters in this category would include:

(i) Powers Related to American Sovereignty, Defence and External Relations

- international/diplomatic relations and foreign policy (this would not omit Gullah/Geechee missions related to maintaining contact in exchanges with states related to the Gullah/Geechee interest, religion or language)
- national defence and security
- security of national borders
- international treaty-making (except where such a treaty may be of particular concern to the cultural preservation of the Gullah/Geechee community)
- immigration, naturalization and aliens (except where it is concerned with becoming a citizen of the Gullah/Geechee nation; a citizen of the Gullah/Geechee nation needs always to be a citizen of the U.S.)
- international trade, including tariffs and import/export controls

(ii) Other National Interest Powers

- management and regulation of the national economy, including:
  - regulation of the national business framework, fiscal and monetary policy
  - a central bank and the banking system
  - bankruptcy and insolvency
  - trade and competition policy
  - intellectual property
  - incorporation of federal corporations
  - currency
- maintenance of national law and order and substantive criminal law, including:
  - offences and penalties under the Criminal Code and other criminal laws
  - emergencies and the "peace, order and good government" power
- protection of the health and safety of all Americans
- federal undertakings and other powers, including:
  - broadcasting and telecommunications
  - aeronautics
  - navigation and shipping
  - maintenance of national transportation systems
  - postal service
  - census and statistics

While law-making power in these areas will not be the subject of negotiations, the Government must be prepared to consider administrative arrangements where it might be feasible and appropriate, or to negotiate a special role for Gullah/Geechee courts or sentencing circles, national telecommunications networks, a development bank, etc.

Mechanisms for Implementation

The Gullah/Geechee Council of Elders (Wisdom Circle) anticipates that agreements on self-determination will be given effect through a variety of mechanisms including negotiated agreements, special measures, legislation, contracts and non-binding memoranda of understanding.

Special Measures

The Government of the United States must be prepared, where the other parties agree, to constitutionally protect rights set out in negotiated self-determination agreements within the meaning of Article 27 of the International Covenant on Civil and Political Rights. Implementation of the human right to self-determination in this fashion would represent a continuation in the progress of the historic relationship between the Gullah/Geechee people and the government which began as one of enslavement and moved through the Apartheid Era, the Civil Rights Era, and now towards the Self-determination Era.

Such agreements will create mutually binding obligations and commitments which would be legally or constitutionally protected. Recognizing the solemn and enduring nature of such agreements, the Council believes that the primary criterion for determining whether or not a matter should receive legal or constitutional protection is whether it is a fundamental element of self-determination that should bind future generations. Under this approach, suitable matters for legal or constitutional protection would include:

- a listing of jurisdictions or authorities by subject matter and related arrangements;
- the relationship of Gullah/Geechee laws to federal and state laws;
- the geographic Gullah/Geechee population areas within which the Gullah/Geechee government or institution will exercise its jurisdiction or authority, and the people to be affected thereby; and
- matters relating to the accountability of the Gullah/Geechee government to its members, in order to establish its legitimacy and the legitimacy of its laws.

It follows from this approach that matters in agreements of a technical or temporary nature would not be appropriate matters for constitutional protection. Arrangements that must be adaptable to changing circumstances, such as program and service delivery arrangements, and funding arrangements, would therefore not be appropriate subjects for constitutional protection.

Legislation, Contracts and Memoranda of Understanding, Special Measures (Negotiated Agreements)

Self-determination arrangements will not be implemented exclusively through special measures. Other mechanisms that will play a role in this process include legislation, contracts and non-binding memoranda of understanding. Legislation can be used in the following ways:

- to ratify and give effect to special measures;
- to implement particular provisions of special measures; and
- to act as a stand-alone mechanism when the parties concerned wish to implement self-determination arrangements, but not through special measures.

Legally enforceable contracts can be used for setting out detailed, technical or time-limited agreements respecting the implementation of self-determination arrangements. Finally, memoranda of understanding, which are not legally enforceable, may also be used to set out political commitments on self-determination.

Existing Territorial Agreements

The Government must be willing to look into existing land claims demands by such organizations as the Gullah/Geechee Sea Island Coalition, etc. within the context of implementing self-determination in this Agreement.

Within this policy framework, the state government should be prepared to negotiate self-determination agreements with those Gullah/Geechee groups who live in the same areas wherein they form 50% or more of the population, and are presently practicing self-determination but do not have self-determination agreements.

Application of Laws

As a right which is exercised within the framework of the American Constitution, the human right to self-determination will not lead to the automatic exclusion of federal and state laws, many of which will continue to apply to Gullah/Geechees or will co-exist alongside validly enacted Gullah/Geechee laws.

To minimize the possibility of conflicts between Gullah/Geechee laws and federal or state laws, the Council of Elders believes that all agreements, including special measures, should establish rules of priority by which such conflicts can be resolved. The Council of Elders takes the position that negotiated rules of priority may provide for the paramountcy of Gullah/Geechee laws, but may not deviate from the basic principle that those federal and state laws of overriding national or state importance will prevail over conflicting Gullah/Geechee laws. Prior to the conclusion of self-determination agreements, federal and state laws would continue to apply to the extent that they do currently.

Transition

It will be important to ensure a smooth transition from current arrangements to implementation of the human right to self-determination through negotiated agreements. All agreements, including special measures, should therefore include appropriate transition measures to ensure that implementation of self-determination does not create legal uncertainty.

The Council appreciates that certain Black individuals assumed to be Gullah/Geechees may not wish to be under Gullah/Geechee jurisdiction or that they may wish to remain in whatever jurisdiction they are presently in. Also, some Gullah/Geechee groups may not wish to exercise as full a range of jurisdiction or authority as others immediately, in which case the current legislative regime will continue to apply until self-determination agreements have been negotiated. Alternatively, some groups may want to structure their self-determination agreements so that some jurisdictions or authorities can be taken up immediately and others exercised in a phased manner, in accordance with the group's needs, capacities and preferred timetable. In this case, the current legislative regime should continue to apply in relation to those jurisdictions or authorities that have not yet been taken up pursuant to a negotiated agreement.

Jurisdiction or Authority Over Non-Members

Negotiations with Gullah/Geechee groups residing on a land base must address the rights and interests of non-members residing on Gullah/Geechee lands. Agreements should indicate clearly if Gullah/Geechee jurisdiction or authority will be exercised over non-members. Where the exercise of Gullah/Geechee jurisdiction or authority over non-members is contemplated, agreements must provide for the establishment of mechanisms through which non-members may have input into decisions that will affect their rights and interests, and must provide for rights of redress.

Fiduciary Obligations

As Gullah/Geechee governments and institutions will exercise jurisdiction or authority and assume control over decision-making that affects sectors of their communities, they will also assume greater responsibilities for the exercise of those powers. As a result, the U.S. state and federal government responsibilities will lessen but not disappear. As the historic relationship between the Gullah/Geechee people and the Anglo-Carolinian people will evolve from one of complete socio-political and economic dependence towards one of interdependence as a natural consequence both of Gullah/Geechees' changing role in shaping their own lives and communities, and enlarging the institutions and developmental scope of an equal status relationship.

In circumstances where Gullah/Geechees wish the U.S. or state government to have certain ongoing obligations, self-determination jurisdiction or authority will, correspondingly, be limited. In such cases, continuing American government obligations should be clearly defined. There is no justifiable basis for the Government to retain fiduciary obligations in relation to subject matters over which it has relinquished its control and over which a Gullah/Geechee government or institution has, correspondingly, assumed control (over which the Gullah/Geechee government or taxation authority applies). Thus political authority will be directly related to fiduciary responsibilities.

Accountability

Gullah/Geechee governments and institutions should be fully accountable to their members or citizens for all of their jurisdiction or authority. Mechanisms to ensure political and financial accountability should be comparable to those in place for other levels of governments and institutions of similar size, although they need not be identical in all respects.

Mechanisms to ensure political accountability are being developed, ratified and set out in the Gullah/Geechee constitution so that they are transparent to all members, and to others who deal with the Gullah/Geechee governments or institutions. In determining the specific accountability measures required, consideration will need to be given to the particular functions of Gullah/Geechee autonomous governing structures and institutions, such as the exercise of jurisdiction, the delivery of programs and services, and/or the administration and enforcement of regulations.

Gullah/Geechee governments exercising law-making authority will establish:

- clear and open processes of law-making;
- transparent processes for proclaiming a law in effect;
- procedures for the notification and publication of laws; and
- procedures for the appeal of laws or other decisions.

Gullah/Geechee institutions exercising authorities will:

- ensure that the decision-making processes central to the core functions of those institutions are open and transparent;
- ensure that information on administrative policies and standards is readily obtainable by clients; and
- establish procedures, where appropriate, for administrative review, including appeal mechanisms.

This is required as the basis for equal status integration, or voluntary assimilation without oppression and discrimination.

Mechanisms to ensure administrative and financial accountability to members and to clients will also be established, and should be no less stringent than those existing for other governments and institutions of comparable size. Such mechanisms will respect the principles of transparency, disclosure and redress.

Financial records and statements will comply with generally accepted accounting principles for governments and institutions of comparable size. In addition, public accounts must be prepared and made available, and provision must be made for annual public audits of expenditures.

Gullah/Geechee governments and institutions must also be accountable to the state legislature or to Congress for funding provided by the federal government as a result of self-determination agreements. Specifically, financing agreements will provide for a mechanism enabling the state or Congress to assess the extent to which public funds have contributed to the objectives for which they were voted.

Gullah/Geechee governments and institutions will develop rules with respect to conflict of interest for both elected and appointed officials. In particular, conflict-of-interest rules will ensure that services that provide an opportunity for financial gain operate at arm's length from elected and appointed officials.

Financial Arrangements

The Government's position should be that financing self-determination is a shared responsibility among federal, state and local governments, and Gullah/Geechee governments and institutions. Specific financing arrangements will be negotiated among governments and each Gullah/Geechee authority concerned.

The Government would normally require that an agreement on cost-sharing between the federal government and the relevant state or local government be secured prior to the commencement of substantive negotiations. In negotiating new financial arrangements and cost-sharing agreements, the federal government would maintain the position that it has primary but not exclusive responsibility; the cost of Gullah/Geechees' self-determination should be shared by the states.

All participants in self-determination negotiations must recognize that self-determination arrangements will have to be affordable and consistent with the overall social and economic policies and priorities of government, while at the same time taking into account the specific needs of Gullah/Geechees. In this regard, the fiscal and budgetary capacity of the federal, state, municipal and Gullah/Geechee governments or institutions will be a primary determinant of the financing of self-determination.

Specific financial arrangements for the financing of Gullah/Geechee governments and institutions should take into account, among other factors:

- the shared objective of ensuring the comparability of basic public services for Gullah/Geechees to those available to other Americans in the vicinity (comparability does not mean that programs, services or funding must be identical in all cases);
- the need for reasonably stable, predictable and flexible funding arrangements for Gullah/Geechee governments and institutions;

- existing levels of support provided by governments;
- the jurisdictions, authorities, programs and services to be assumed by Gullah/Geechee governments or institutions;
- the Gullah/Geechee group's ability to raise its own-source revenues, and other resources available to it; and
- the efficiency and cost-effectiveness of the proposed arrangements, including issues related to the size, location and accessibility of the groups.

In addition, financial arrangements should be consistent with principles of sound public administration.

In the present climate of scarce resources it will be particularly important for the various levels of government to work together to harmonize funding, programs and service delivery arrangements, thereby ensuring the most efficient and effective use of state and national resources. The Council expects that, wherever feasible, Gullah/Geechee governments and institutions will develop their own sources of revenue in order to reduce reliance, over time, on transfers from other levels of government.

Non-Duplication of Access to Programs

Gullah/Geechee communities and individuals covered by self-determination arrangements will continue to be eligible for programs that the federal government may establish from time to time. However, where a comparable jurisdiction, authority or program has been assumed by a Gullah/Geechee authority pursuant to a special measures agreement, individuals under that Gullah/Geechee authority would not ordinarily be eligible for similar federal programs.

Implementation Plans

The Government should require a separate implementation plan for all self-determination agreements to be approved in conjunction with Final Agreements. Implementation plans must identify the activities, timeframes and resources that have been agreed upon to give effect to the agreements. Issues related to affordability, efficiency, capital requirements, duplication of services, feasibility and capacity will have to be addressed.

The Government will of course have to recognize that there will be new costs associated with the transition from the existing regime to implementation of new self-determination arrangements. Therefore there will not be a separate source of funding for implementation and transition costs. All such costs will have to be provided for by the government, the UN, or governmental aid to the Gullah/Geechees (African American restorative development)

In addition, self-determination agreements may not include any program enrichment. Any decisions by the federal government regarding program enrichment would have to be made within the context of that program and by the department concerned, not as a consequence of self-determination agreements. Once self-determination arrangements are in place, however, Gullah/Geechee governments will be free to redirect and redistribute monies into those areas they deem appropriate, subject to maintaining whatever statutory requirements and minimal standards of program and service delivery that have been agreed upon.

PART II: VARIOUS APPROACHES TO SELF-DETERMINATION

The Government should recognize that the Gullah/Geechees in the various communities of the South, North, West, etc. have different needs, circumstances and aspirations, and want to exercise their human right in different ways. Some want their own governments on their land base; some may want to work within wider social service and public government structures; and some want institutional arrangements. The Government is prepared to support various approaches, taking into account differing needs and circumstances, and to be flexible on the specific arrangements which may be negotiated.

Many Gullah/Geechees have expressed a strong desire to control their own affairs and communities, and deliver programs and services better tailored to their own values and cultures. They want to replace the policy of forced assimilation and cultural rejection with one of pride in cultural preservation in the context of an equal-status integration.

The Government of the United States should be prepared to work with all Gullah/Geechee groups to address these aspirations. The Government should hold that its approach to implementing the human right will allos Gullah/Geechees and governments to establish mutually satisfactory negotiation processes leading to agreements that will recognize their human dignity and right to have control over their communities and development. Finally, where the parties to negotiations agree, the Government should be prepared to protect rights contained in negotiated self-determination agreements as constitutionally protected rights.

The Government should also be prepared to constitutionally protect rights negotiated in public institutional arrangements where appropriate and if the parties to the negotiations agree. Such negotiations would necessarily include the state and municipal governments (its public institutions) in order to ensure harmonious intergovernmental relationships.

Self-determination arrangements in a public government context do not preclude consideration of other arrangements at some future date, provided that all parties concerned are in agreement.

Government should accept that the onus to resolve any disputes regarding representation within or among Gullah/Geechee people should rest with the Gullah/Geechee people.

Role of Municipalities and Third Parties

Recognizing the importance of conducting negotiations in a spirit of openness and co-operation, the Government should be committed to providing municipalities and third parties with meaningful opportunities to have input into negotiation processes that may directly affect their interests. To this end, the Government will work with the states, municipalities and Gullah/Geechee groups to develop appropriate consultation mechanisms for municipalities and third parties that may be directly affected by self-determination negotiations and agreements.

Approval of Negotiated Agreements (Special Measures) for the Gullah/ Geechee national minority

Within the government, executive approval should be sought for Agreements-in-Principle and Final Agreements, and legislative approval sought for negotiated self-determination agreements and any implementing legislation that may be required.

The Government should require evidence that negotiated agreements have been ratified by the Gullah/Geechee people in a way that demonstrates clearly the people's consent. While the specific ratification mechanism can be negotiated, it will have to ensure that all members have an opportunity to participate, that they have all relevant information available, and that the procedures for ratification are transparent and recognized as binding.

APPENDIX D

Commentary to the Declaration on Prevention of Discrimination and Protection of Minorities

Asbjorn Eide*

COMMISSION ON HUMAN RIGHTS
Sub-Commission on Promotion and Protection of Human Rights
Working Group on Minorities
Sixth session, 22-26 May 2000

COMMENTARY TO THE DECLARATION ON THE RIGHTS OF PERSONS BELONGING TO NATIONAL OR ETHNIC, RELIGIOUS AND LINGUISTIC MINORITIES

Working paper submitted by Asbjørn Eide

I. Introduction

At its third session held in May 1997 the Working Group on Minorities recommended the preparation of a commentary or a guide to the interpretation of the Declaration on the Rights of Persons belonging to National or Ethnic, Religious and Linguistic Minorities adopted by the General Assembly in December 1992. In my capacity as Chairman I prepared an initial draft for discussion and comments . It was discussed at the fourth session of the Working Group in 1998, and subsequently circulated to governments, intergovernmental and nongovernmental organizations and individual experts for comments. A compilation of those comments were submitted to the fifth session of the Working Group in 1999 . Several additional comments for further improvement were made during that session, whereupon the Working Group requested me to prepare a

* UN Doc. E/CN.4/Sub.2/AC.5/2000/WP.1, April 27, 2000. A listing of papers of the former UN Working Group on Minorities and the present Independent Expert on minority issues as well as the pamphlets in the UN Guide for Minorities by theme, by country/region and major studies or reports of the former UN Sub-Commission is available at <http://www2.ohchr.org/english/issues/minorities/docs/docstable.doc>

final draft for its sixth session. The present version draws, in addition to my own studies, on the written work or oral contributions by many experts, governments, international and non-governmental organisations .

II. Purposes of the Declaration: advancing human rights and the principles of the UN Charter

The aims of the Declaration of 1992 are set out in its preamble. It starts by reaffirming that the promotion and encouragement of respect for human rights is a basic aim of the United Nations. The Minority Declaration is intended to contribute to the realization of the principles of the Charter of the United Nations and those of the human rights instruments adopted at the universal or regional level. The Declaration is inspired by Article 27 of the International Covenant on Civil and Political Rights. The promotion and protection of rights of minorities should contribute to the political and social stability of the states in which minorities live, and to the strengthening of friendship and co-operation among peoples and states. Recognizing that the United Nations has an important role to play regarding the protection of minorities, more effective implementation of international human rights instruments is required with regard to persons belonging to minorities.

In sum, therefore the Declaration is intended to strengthen the implementation of human rights in so far as minorities are concerned, within the context of the principles of the United Nations Charter, in the pursuit of political and social stability and international peace.

The Declaration builds on but adds to the rights contained in the International Bill of Human Rights and other human rights instruments by strengthening and clarifying those rights which make it possible for persons belonging to minorities to preserve and develop their group identity. The foundational principles of human rights must at all times be respected in the process. One of those foundational principles is that of non-discrimination between individuals. The state is obliged to respect and ensure to every person within its territory and subject to its jurisdiction, without discrimination on any ground including race, ethnicity, religion or national origin, the rights contained in the instruments to which that state is a party. It is in the light of these principles that the articles of the Minority Declaration must be interpreted.

III. Interpretation of, and comments to, the title and the individual articles

The title and the scope of the Declaration

'Declaration on the Rights of Persons belonging to National or Ethnic, Religious or Linguistic Minorities'

The scope of Article 27 of the International Covenant on Civil and Political Rights, which has inspired the Declaration, are 'ethnic, religious or linguistic minorities'. The 1992 Declaration adds 'national minorities'. That addition does not extend the scope of application beyond the groups covered by Article 27. While there is no agreement on what 'national minority' means in distinction to, e.g. an ethnic minority, there is hardly any national minority, however defined, that is not also an ethnic or linguistic or linguistic minority.

The addition of 'national minority' can only have a significance if it is assumed that different kinds of minorities have different rights. It can be argued that persons belonging to religious minorities have only those special rights which relate to the profession and practice of their religion, that persons belonging to linguistic minorities have only those special rights which are related to the learning and use of their language, and ethnic minorities have wider rights related to the preservation and development of their culture. If so, it might be argued that persons belonging to national minorities have even stronger rights related to the preservation and development of their national identity.

It is doubtful, however, whether such an inference can be made. There are several and quite different understandings of 'national minority'. One understanding is simply that a national minority is one which has existed in the state for some time and is composed of citizens of that state. If that is the understanding, it is not different from any other ethnic or linguistic minority except for its length of existence and the requirement of citizenship. Another understanding of a 'national minority' is that it forms part of a larger ethno-nation, for instance one which forms the majority in a neigbouring kin-state.

In the absence of agreement on the concept of 'national minority' one is probably best served, however, by avoiding to give any special significance to that category. There are other factors which can be relevant in distinguishing between the rights that can be demanded by different minorities: Those who live compactly together in the part of a territory may be entitled to rights regarding the use of language, street and place names which are different from those who live dispersed, and those who have existed for a long time in the territory may have stronger rights than those who have recently arrived. Persons belonging to groups which are large may have stronger rights than those whose group is tiny.

In the drafting of the Declaration no consensus was achieved on the definition of minorities. As it is inspired by Article 27 of the Covenant, it may be assumed that the Declaration has at least as wide a scope as that article. Taking into account the views expressed in General Comment of the Human Rights Committee No.23 para. 5.1 and 5.2 (50th sesssion, 1994) and the arguments on which it was based, this would imply that persons who are not (yet) citizens of the country in which they reside can form part or belong to a minority in that country. On the other hand, the rights contained in the Declaration are somewhat stronger than the minimum rights which can be derived from CCPR Article 27, and this might justify a more limited scope for the Declaration than for Article 27. The best approach appears to be to avoid making a strict distinction between 'new' and 'old' minorities, but to recognize that in the application of the Declaration the 'old' minorities have stronger entitlements than the 'new'.

The word 'minority' can sometimes be misleading in itself. Outside Europe, and particularly in Africa. countries are often composed of a large number of groups, none of which make up a majority. The factors may differ significantly between states. What is required is to ensure appropriate rights for members of all groups and to develop good governance in heterogenous societies which allows for peaceful and constructive group accomodation based on equality in dignity and rights for all.

The Declaration sets out rights of persons belonging to minorities (mainly in Article 2) and the duties of the states in which they exist (particularly in Articles 1, 4 and 5). While the rights are consistently set out as rights of individuals, the duties of states are in part formulated as duties towards minorities as groups, particularly in Article 1. While only individuals can claim the rights, the state cannot fully implement them without ensuring adequate conditions for the existence and identity of the group as a whole.

The rights of persons belonging to minorities differ from the rights of peoples to self-determination. While the latter right is well established under international law, in particular common Article 1 to the two International Covenants on Human Rights, the scope of the right and the meaning of the concepts of 'people' and 'self-determination' is still ambiguous and highly controversial. This point has no impact on the Minority Declaration, since there is no disagreement that rights of persons belonging to minorities are individual rights, even if they in most cases can only be enjoyed in community with others. The rights of peoples, on the other hand, are collective rights.

Within the United Nations and also within the Organization of American States, a distinction is increasingly drawn between the rights of persons belonging to minorities and those of the rights of indigenous peoples. The latter have particular concerns which are not properly addressed in the Minority Declaration. The main instrument at the global level concerning indigenous peoples is the ILO Convention 169 Concerning Indigenous and Tribal Peoples in Sovereing Countries, which has been ratified only by a small number of states. The draft declaration adopted by the Working Group on Indigenous Populations and transmitted by the Sub-Commission on Prevention of Discrimination and Protection of Minorities in 1993 to the Commission on Human Rights is still under consideration in the Commission.

Persons belonging to indigenous peoples are fully entitled, if they so wish, to claim the rights contained in the minority instruments. This has repeatedly been done under Article 27 of the Covenant on Civil and Political Rights. Persons belonging to indigenous peoples have made several submissions under the first optional protocol to that Covenant. The latter does not generally make it possible to demand the group-oriented rights of indigenous peoples, but General Comment No.23 of the Human Rights Committee (50th session, 1994) para. 7 should here be taken into account. The Committee notes that especially in the case of indigenous peoples the preservation of their use of land resources can become an essential element in the right of persons belonging to such minorities to exercise their cultural rights.

Some see a link between the right for persons belonging to minorities to effective political participation and the right of peoples to self-determination. The issue of effective participation is addressed below, in the comments to Article 2.2 and 2.3. Suffice it here to note that self-determination, if taken literally, is the opposite of participation, since it is a claim of non-participation combined with a claim of non-subordination.

Denial of reasonably effective participation to which persons belonging to minorities are entitled might in some cases be used as an argument by a group which collectively argues that it constitutes a people and therefore is entitled to self-determination. The pursuit of that right would have to be done outside the framework of the Minority Declaration. If the group concerned, in claiming a right to self-determination, challenges the territorial integrity of the state, it follows explicitly from Article 8 para.4 that this cannot be based on the Minority Declaration. The same would apply in other contexts where the collective right to self-determination is made. The Minority Declaration neither limits nor extends the rights that peoples have under other parts of international law to self-determination.

While the Declaration does not provide group rights of self-determination, the duties of the state to protect the identity of minorities may include a duty to accept and encourage conditions for extensive autonomy in regard to religious, linguistic or broader cultural matters. Such autonomies can be organized and managed by associations set up by persons belonging to minorities in accordance with Article 2.4.

Article 1

1.1 States shall protect the existence and the national or ethnic, cultural, religious and linguistic identity of minorities within their respective territories and shall encourage conditions for the promotion of that identity.

The relationship between the State and its minorities has in the past taken five different forms: elimination, assimilation, toleration, protection and promotion. The Declaration is based on the consideration that elimination is clearly illegal and that at least forced assimilation is also unacceptable. It seeks to go beyond toleration to move towards protection and promotion.

A degree of integration is required in every national society. Without out it, the conditions for the functioning of civil society would not exist, nor would it be possible for the state to respect and ensure human rights to every person within its territory without discrimination. The protection of minorities, however, is intended to ensure that integration does not become unwanted assimilation; that it does not undermine the group identity of persons belonging to the different groups living on the territory of the state. Integration differs fundamentally from assimilation. Integration consists in the development and maintenance of a common domain where equal treatment and a common rule of law prevails, while allowing for pluralism in the areas covered by the

Declaration: Culture, language and religion. Minority protection is therefore based on four requirements: Protection of their existence, non-exclusion, non-discrimination and non-assimilation.

The first requirement is to protect the existence of minorities. This includes their physical existence, their continued existence on the territories on which the minorities live, and the continued access to the material resources required to continue their existence on those territories. They shall neither be physically excluded from the territory nor be excluded from access to the resources required for their livelihood. The right to existence in its physical sense is sustained by the Convention on the Prevention and Punishment of the Crime of Genocide, which codified customary law in 1948. Forced population transfers intended or with the effect to move persons belonging to minorities away from the territory on which they live would constitute serious breaches of contemporary international standards, including the statutes of the International Criminal Court. Protection of their existence goes beyond the duty not to destroy or deliberately weaken the minority group. It also requires respect for and protection of their religious and cultural heritage essential to their group identity, including buildings and sites such as libraries, churches, mosques, temples, synagogues and the like.

The second requirement is that minorities shall not be excluded from the national society. Apartheid was the extreme version of exclusion of different groups from equal participation in the national society as a whole. The minority Declaration repeatedly underlines the rights of all groups, small as well as large, to participate effectively in society (Article 2.2 and 2.3)

The third requirement is non-discrimination, which is a general principle of human rights law and elaborated i.a. by the International Convention on the Elimination of All Forms of Racial Discrimination. The latter also covers discrimination on ethnic grounds. The Minority Declaration elaborates the principle of non-discrimination by its provision that the exercise of their rights as persons belonging to minorities shall not justify any discrimination in any other field, and that no disadvantage shall result from the exercose or non-exercise of these rights (Article 3).

The fourth requirement is non-assimilation and its corollary, which is to protect and promote conditions for the group identity of minorities. Many recent international instruments use the term 'identity', which expresses a clear trend towards the protection and promotion of cultural diversity both internationally and internally to states. Relevant provisions are Articles 29 and 30 of the Convention on the Rights of the Child, Article 31 of the UN Migrant Workers Convention, Article 2(2)(b) of ILO Convention No. 169, which refers to respect for the social and cultural identity, customs and traditions and institutions of indigenous peoples, as well as in regional instruments such as the Organisation on Security and Cooperation in Europe, including its 1990 Copenhagen Human Dimen¬sion Confer¬ence and its Geneva Meeting of Experts on National Minorities 1991. Another recent document in the same direction is the European Framework Convention for the Protection of Minorities.

Identity is essentially cultural, and requires not only tolerance but a positive attitude of cultural pluralism by the state and the larger society. Required is not only acceptance but also respect for the distinctive characteristics and contri¬bution of minor¬ities in the life of the national society as a whole. Protection of the identity means not only that the state shall abstain from policies which have the purpose or effect of assimilating the minorities into the dominant culture, but also that it shall protect them against activities by third parties which have assimilatory effect. Crucial in these regards are the language policies and the educational policies of the state concerned. Denying minorities the possibility to learn their own language or instruction in their own language, or excluding from the education of minorities transmission of knowledge about their own culture, history, tradition and language, would be a violation of the obligation to protect their identity.

Promotion of their identity requires special measures intended to facilitate the maintenance, reproduction and further development of the culture of the minorities. Cultures are not static, but minorities should be given the opportunity to develop their own culture in the context of an ongoing process. It should be an interaction between the persons belonging to the minority themselves, between the minority and the state, and between the minority and the wider national society. The measures required to achieve this purpose are set out in greater detail in article 4 of the Declaration.

1.2 States shall adopt appropriate legislative and other measures to achieve those ends.

Article 1(2) requires 'appropriate legislative and other measures'. Legislation is required and must be complemented by other measures in order to ensure that Article 1 can be effectively implemented. Both process and content is here important. In terms of process, it is essential that the state consult the minorities on what would constitute appropriate measures. This follows also from Article 2(3) of the Declaration. Different minorities may have different needs that must be taken into account. Any differences in policy, however, must be based on objective and reasonable grounds in order to avoid discrimination.

Other measures include judicial, administrative, promptional, educational and further policies and measures.

In general terms, the content of the measures which have to be adopted are set out in the other provisions of the Declaration, particularly Articles 2 and 4, which will be discussed below. One set of measures follow directly from Article 1(1): States must adopt laws protecting against acts or the incitement to such acts which threaten the existence of groups physically or their identity. This obligation follows also from the International Convention on the Elimination of All Forms of Racial Discrimination, which also includes ethnic discrimination, and from the International Covenant on Civil and Political Rights. In accordance with Article 4 of the Racial Convention, states must adopt legislative measures intended to protect groups against hatred and violence on national or ethnic, racial, religious and linguistic grounds. Article 2

2.1 Persons belonging to national or ethnic, religious and linguistic minorities (hereinafter referred to as persons belonging to minorities) have the right to enjoy their own culture, to profess and practice their own religion, and to use their own language, in private and in public, freely and without interference or any form of discrimination.

Article 27 of the International Covenant on Civil and Political Rights has almost the same language, but the Declaration has taken one step further. Under Article 27, the language used is that the persons belonging to the minorities "shall not be denied the right", whereas the Declaration of 1992 uses the positive term that they "have the right". While Article 27 has been interpreted by the Human Rights Committee to go beyond mere passive non-interference, the formulation in the Minority Declaration makes it clear that these rights often require action, including protective measures and promotion of the condition for their identity (Article 1). Article 4 also requires specified, active measures by the state.

Therefore, it is not enough that the state abstains from interference or discrimination, it must also ensure that individuals and organisations of the larger society do not interfere or discriminate. This principle follows from the words "freely and without interference or any form of discrimination".

2.2 Persons belonging to minorities have the right to participate effectively in cultural, religious, social, economic and public life.

While persons belonging to minorities have the right to preserve their own group identity, they also have a right to participate in all aspects of the life of the larger national society. This right is essential both in order for persons belonging to minorities to promote their interests and values and to create an integrated but pluralist society based on tolerance and dialogue. By their participation in all forms of public life in their country, they are able both to shape their own destinies and to contribute to the political evolution in the larger society.

The words "public life" must be understood in the same broad sense as in ICERD Article 1, though much is covered already by the preceding words 'cultural, religious, social and economic..' Additionally included in 'public life' are, among others, rights related to election and to be elected, the holding of public office, and other political and administrative domains.

Participation can be ensured in many ways, including the use of minority associations (see also Article 2.4), membership in other associations, and through their free contacts both inside the state and across borders (see Article 2.5)

2.3 Persons belonging to minorities have the right to participate effectively in decisions on the national, and where appropriate, regional level concerning the minority to which they belong or the regions in which they live, in a manner not incompatible with national legislation.

While Article 2.2 deals generally with the right to participation in all aspects of public life in society, Article 2.3 deals specifically with the right of persons belonging to minorities to effective participation 'in decisions... ..concerning the minority to which they belong or the regions in which they live'. As such decisions have a particular impact on themselves, the emphasis on effective participation is here of particular importance. Representatives of persons belonging to minorities should be involved already from the initial stages of decision-making. Experience has shown that it is of little use to involve them only at the final stages where there is very little room for compromise. Minorities should be involved at the local, national and international level in the formulation, adoption, implementation and monitoring of standards and policies affecting them.

In 1991, the Conference on Security and Co-operation in Europe held a Meeting of Experts on National Minorities in Geneva. The states there assembled noted approaches used with positive results in some of the partici¬pating states. These included advisory and decision-making bodies in which minorities are represented, in particular with regard to education, culture and religion. Mentioned was also assemblies of national minority affairs; local and autonomous administration, as well as autonomy on a territorial basis, including the exist¬ence of consultative, legislative and executive bodies chosen through free and periodic elections. Reference was further made to forms of self-administration by a nation¬al minority of aspects concerning its identity in situations where autonomy on a terri¬torial basis does not apply; and decentralized or local forms of government .

In early May 1999, a group of independent experts met in Lund, Sweden to draw up a set of recommendations on the effective participation of national minorities in public life. The recommendations are built upon fundamental principles and rules of international law, such as respect for human dignity, equal rights, and non-discrimination, as they affect the rights of national minorities to participate in public life and to enjoy other political rights. At its fifth session at the end of May 1999, the Working Group on Minorities of the Sub-Commission on Prevention of Discrimination and Protection of Minorities adopted a set of recommendations on the same topic, drawn in part from a seminar on the theme of minority participation organised for the Working Group by the European Centre for Minority Issues (ECMI) in Flensburg in April 1999.

The following commentary draws extensively on the insight gained from these encounters. The purpose is not simply to set out the minimum rights of persons belonging to minorities under Article 2.3, but also to list a set of good practices which may be of use for governments and minorities in finding appropriate solutions to issues confronting them. More detailed recommendations can be found, in particular, in the Lund Recommendations on the Effective Participation of National Minorities in Public Life.

Effective participation provides channels for consultation between and among minorities and governments. It can serve as means of dispute resolution and sustain diversity as a condition for dynamic stability of society. Since the numbers of minorities by definition are too small to determine the outcome, it is required as a minimum that persons belonging to minorities have the right to have their opinions heard and fully taken into account before decisions which concern them are adopted. A wide range of constitutional and political measures is used around the world to provide access for minorities to decision-making.

The variety in composition, needs and aspirations of different types of minority groups require identification and adoption of the most appropriate ways to create conditions for effective participation in each case. The mechanisms chosen have to take into account whether the persons belonging to the minority in question live dispersed or in compactly settled groups, whether the minority is small or large, or an old or a new minority. Religious minorities may also require different types or contexts of participation than ethnic or national minorities. It should be noted, however, that in some cases the religion and ethnicity coincide.

Effective participation requires representation in legislative, administrative and advisory bodies and more generally in public life. Persons belonging to minorities, like all others, are entitled to assemble and to form their associations, and thereby to aggregate their interests and values to make the greatest possible impact on national and regional decision-making. They are entitled not only to set up and make use of ethnic, cultural and religious associations and societies (see commentary to Article 2.4 below), but also political parties, should they so wish. In a well integrated society, however, many persons belonging to minorities often prefer to be members of or vote for parties which are not organized on ethnic lines but are sensitive to the concerns of the minorities.

Where minorities are concentrated territorially, single-member districts may provide sufficient minority representation. Proportional representation systems, where a political party's share in the national vote is reflected in its share of the legislative seats, may assist in the representation of minorities. Some forms of preference voting, where voters rank candidates in order of choice, may also facilitate minority representation and promote inter-communal co-operation.

Decentralisation of powers based on the principle of subsidiarity, whether called self-government or devolved power, and whether the arrangements are symmetrical or asymmetrical, would increase the chances of minorities to participate in the exercise of authority over matters affecting themselves and the entire societies in which they live.

Public institutions should not, however, be based on ethnic or religious criteria. Governments at local, regional and national levels should recognise the role of multiple identities in contributing to open communities and in establishing useful distinctions between public institutional structures and cultural identities.

States should also establish advisory or consultative bodies involving minorities within appropriate institutional frameworks. Such bodies or roundtables should be attributed political weight and effectively consulted on issues affecting the minority population.

There should be equal access to public sector employment across the various ethnic, linguistic and religious communities.

Citizenship remains an important condition for full and effective participation. Barriers to the acquisition of citizenship for members of minorities should be reduced. Forms of participation by resident non-citizens should also be developed, including local voting rights after a certain period of residence and inclusion of elected non-citizen observers in municipal, regional and national legislative and decision-making assemblies.

2.4 Persons belonging to minorities have the right to establish and maintain their own associations.

Persons belonging to minorities are entitled, in the same way as other members of society, to set up any association they may want. These may include educational or religious institutions, but their right to association is not limited to those related to their cultural, linguistic or religious identity. The right to associate extends both to national and to international associations. Their right to form or join associations can be limited only by law, and the limitations can only be those which apply to associations of majorities: limitations must be necessary in a democratic society in the interests of national security or public safety, public order, the protection of public health or morals or the protection of the rights and freedoms.

2.5 Persons belonging to minorities have the right to establish and maintain, without any discrimination, free and peaceful contacts with other members of their group and with persons belonging to other minorities, as well as contacts across frontiers with citizens of other states to whom they are related by national or ethnic, religious or linguistic ties.

The right to contacts has three facets, permitting intra-minority contacts; inter-minority contacts; and transfrontier contacts. The right to intra-minority contacts is inherent in the right to association. The inter-minority contacts make it possible for persons belonging to minorities to share experience and information and to develop a common minority platform
within the state. The right to transfrontier contacts constitute the major innovation of the Declaration, and serves in part to overcome some of the

negative consequences of the often unavoidable division of ethnic groups by international frontiers. Such contacts must be 'free' but also 'peaceful'. The latter limitation has two aspects: It must not involve the use of violent means, of the preparation of such use; secondly, the aims must be in conformity with the Declaration and generally with the purposes and principles of the United Nations, as set out also in Article 8.4 of the Declaration. .
Article 3

3.1 Persons belonging to minorities may exercise their rights, including those set forth in the present Declaration, individually as well as in community with other members of their group, without any discrimination.

The main point here is that persons can exercise their rights both individually and collectively. The most important aspect is the collective exercise of their rights, be it through associations, cultural manifestations or educational institutions, or in any other way. It is never enough for a state to allow for individual use of minority rights, such as an individual's use of her/his own language.

That they can exercise their rights in community with other members of the group apply not only to the rights contained in the Declaration, but any human right. They shall not be subject to any discrimination as a consequence of exercising their rights. This principle is important, because governments or persons belonging to majorities are often tolerant to persons of other national or ethnic origins until such time as the latter assert their own identity, language and tradition. Its when they assert their rights as persons belonging to minorities that discrimination often sets in. Article 3 (1) makes it clear that they shall not be subjected to discrimination for manifesting their group identity.

3.2 No disadvantage shall result for any person belonging to a minority as a consequence of the exercise or non-exercise of the rights set forth in the present Declaration.

While Article 3.1 makes it clear that persons belonging to minorities shall not be subjected to discrimination for exercising, individually or collectively, their minority rights, article 3.2 makes it clear that they shall also not be disadvantaged in any way from choosing not to belong to the minority concerned. This provision is directed both against the state and the agencies of the minority group. The state cannot impose a particular ethnic identity on a given person (which is what the apartheid regime in South Africa sought to do) by the use of negative sanctions against those who do not want to be part of that group; nor can persons belonging to minorities subject to any disadvantage persons who on objective criteria may be held to form part of their group but who subjectively do not want to belong to it. While under conventional law responsibility for human rights compliance normally rests on the state, the Declaration in this respect implies duties – at least morally - also on persons representing minorities. Furthermore, states would be under a duty to prohibit measures taken by minorities to impose their particular rules on persons who do not want to be part of the minority concerned and therefore does not want to exercise her or his rights.

Article 4

The preamble of the Declaration sets out as the main purpose that a more effective implementation of international human rights shall be ensured to persons belonging to national or ethnic, religious and linguistic minorities. Article 4 sets out the state measures that should be taken in order to achieve that purpose. It is, together with Article 2, the most important in the Declaration.

The state must under all circumstances respect and protect the existence of the minority and ensure that its members retain their necessary sources of livelihood, as provided for in Article 1. Furthermore, the state must abstain from any discrimination directed against its members and protect them from discrimination, as set out in Article 4.1 States shall also under all circumstances create favourable conditions to enable persons belonging to minorities to preserve and develop their identity, as set out in Article 4.2. In both respects the word 'shall' is used, indicating a duty. Regarding measures described in Articles 4.3 and 4.4, the degree to which states are able to implement these rights depends on resources available and other factors which differ from country to country, which probably is why the word 'should' is used in those provisions rather than the word 'shall'. What is required is that states seek to implement the rights to the maximum of their available resources and that they seek in good faith to realize the purposes of the Declaration.

4.1 States shall take measures where required to ensure that persons belonging to minorities may exercise fully and effectively their human rights and fundamental freedoms without any discrimination and in full equality before the law.

While states are generally obliged under international law to ensure that all members of society may exercise their human rights, states must give particular attention to the human rights situation of persons belonging to minorities because of the special problems they confront. They are often in a vulnerable position and have in the past often been subjected to discrimination. In order to ensure equality in fact, it may under some circumstances be required that the state take transitional affirmative action as provided in the Race Convention (ICERD) article 2 (2), which is applicable to ethnic as well as racial minorities, provided these measures do not disproportionately affect the rights of others.

4. 2. States shall take measures to create favourable conditions to enable persons belonging to minorities to express their characteristics and to develop their culture, language, religion, traditions and customs, except where specific practices are in violation of national law and contrary to international standards.

The article requires more than mere tolerance of the manifestation of the different cultures within the state. The creation of favourable conditions requires active measures by the state. The nature of those measures depend on the situation of the minority concerned, but should be guided by the purpose set forth in the article, which is twofold: on the one hand, individual members of the minority shall be enabled to express the traditional characteristics of the group, which may include a right to use their traditional dress or attire and to make their living in their own cultural ways. On the other hand, they shall be enabled in community with other persons belonging to the group to further develop their culture, language, traditions and cultures. These measures may require economic resources from the state. In the same way as the state provides funding for the development of the culture and language of the majority, it shall provide resources for similar activities of the minority.

The words 'except where specific practices are in violation of national law and contrary to international standards' require some comments. The meaning of the words 'contrary to international standards' is simple enough. Intended is, in particular, that the practices must not be contrary to international human rights standards. This, however, should apply both to practices both of majorities and minorities. Cultural or religious practices which violate human rights law should be outlawed for everyone, not only for minorities. The qualification contained in the final words of the last sentence of Article 4(2) is therefore only a specific application of a universal principle applicable to everyone.

The first part of the sentence, 'in violation of national law' raises somewhat more difficult questions. It is clear that the state is not free to adopt whatever prohibitions against minorities' cultural practices that it wants. If that was the case, the Declaration and in particular Article 4.2 would be nearly empty of content. What is intended, however, is to respect the margin of appreciation which any state must have regarding which practices it wants to prohibit, taking into account the particular conditions prevailing in that country. As long as the prohibitions are based on reasonable and objective grounds, they must therefore be respected.

4. 3 States should take appropriate measures so that, wherever possible, persons belonging to minorities may have adequate opportunities to learn their mother tongue or to have instructions in their mother tongue.

Language is among the most important carriers of group identity. In line with the general requirement in Article 1 that states shall encourage the promotion of the linguistic identity of the minority concerned, measures are required for persons belonging to minorities to learn their mother tongue (which is a minimum) or to have instruction in their mother tongue (which goes some steps further).

What steps are required in these regards depend on a number of variable factors. Significant will be the size of the group and the nature of its settlement, i.e. whether it lives compactly together or is dispersed throughout the country. It is also of relevance whether it is a long-established minority or a new minority composed of recent immigrants, whether or not these have obtained citizenship.

In cases where the language of the minority is a territorial language traditionally spoken and used by many in a region of the country, states should to the maximum of their available resources ensure that linguistic identity can be preserved. Pre-school and primary school education should ideally in such cases be in the child's own language, i.e. the language of the minority spoken at home. Since persons belonging to minorities like those of the majorities have a duty to integrate into the wider national society, they need also to learn the official or state language(s). The official language(s) should gradually be introduced at later stages. Where there is a large linguistic minority within the country, the language of the minority is sometimes also an official language of the state concerned.

At the European regional level, educational rights relating to language of minorities are developed at greater length in the European Charter for Regional or Minority Languages, adopted by the Council of Europe. A set of recommendations on this subject has been elaborated by a group of experts in the Hague recommendations Regarding the Education Rights of National Minorities, prepared under the auspices of the Foundation on Inter-Ethnic Relations (October 1996).

In regard to non-territorial languages spoken traditionally by a minority within the country but which is not associated with a particular region of that country, a uniform solution is more difficult to find. The same principles as those stated above should be applied where appropriate, but where the persons belonging to the minority live dispersed with only a few persons in each particular place, the child needs at an earlier stage to learn more fully the language of the surrounding environment. Nevertheless, it should always also have an opportunity to learn its mother tongue, In this regard, persons belonging to minorities have a right, like others, to establish their private institutions, where the minority language is the main language of instruction, but the state is entitled to require that the state language is also taught. One question is whether the state is obliged to provide subsidies for such teaching. It would seem required that the state does ensure and fund the existence of some common institutions which can ensure the teaching of that language. It follows from the general wording of Article 4(3) that everyone should have adequate opportunity 'wherever possible'. It would therefore depend on the resources of the state how far the obligation goes to fund education of the minority languages for persons belonging to dispersed groups.

Yet greater difficulties arise in regard to language used solely by persons belonging to new minorities. These are usually more dispersed than are the older and settled minorities, and the number of languages within a country of immigration spoken at home by migrants can be quite large. Furthermore, the child has a great need to learn to use the language of the country of immigration as quickly and as effectively as possible. Should, however, some new minorities settle compactly together in a region of the country and in large number, there is no reason to treat them differently from those of old minorities. It should be noted, however, that the European Charter for Regional or Minority Languages does not cover the languages of migrants. In any case, persons belonging to new minorities are entitled to set up their own private educational institutions where they include the teaching and instruction in their mother tongue and instruction. The state is entitled to demand that the official language is also taught.

4.4 States should, where appropriate, take measures in the field of education, in order to encourage knowledge of the history, traditions, language and culture of the minorities existing within their territory. Persons belonging to minorities should have adequate opportunities to gain knowledge of the society as a whole.

Experience has shown that in societies where different national, ethnic, religious or linguistic groups coexist, the culture, history and traditions of minority groups have often been
neglected, and the majorities are frequently ignorant of those traditions and cultures. Where there has been conflict, the culture, history and traditions have often been subject to distorted represen¬ta¬tions, producing low self-esteem in the groups and negative stereotypes in the wider community. Racial hatred, xenophobia and intolerance sometimes take root.

To avoid such circumstances, there is a need both for multicultural and intercultural education. Multicultural education involves educational policies and practices which meet the separate educational needs of groups in society which belong to different cultural traditions, while intercultural education involves educational policies and practices by which the persons belonging to different cultures, whether in a majority or minority position, learn to interact constructively with each other.

Article 4 calls for intercultural education by the encouragement of knowledge in the society as a whole of the history, tradition and culture of the minorities living there. Cultures and languages of minorities should be made accessible to the majorities as a means to encourage interaction and conflict prevention in pluri-ethnic societies Such knowledge should be presented in a positive way in order to encourage tolerance and respect. History books are particularly important in this regard. Bias in the presentation of the history, and neglect of the contributions of the minority, are significant causes of ethnic tension. UNESCO has been concerned with the need to eliminate such prejudices and misrepresentations in history textbooks, but much remains to be done.

The article also reminds us of the complementary duty to ensure that persons belonging to minorities gain knowledge of the society as a whole. This proviso is to counteract tendencies towards fundamentalist or closed religious or ethnic groups, which can be as much affected by xenophobia and intolerance as the majorities.

The overall purpose of this article is to ensure an egalitarian integration based on non-discrimination and respect for each of the cultural, linguistic or religious groups which together form the national society. The formation of more or less involuntary ghettos where the different groups live in their own world without knowledge of, or tolerance for, the persons belonging to the other parts of the national society, would be a violation of the purpose and spirit of the Declaration.

The concern expressed in Article 4(4) is also found in the International Convention on the Elimination of All forms of Racial Discrimination (article 7) and in the Convention on the Rights of the Child (article 29).

4.5 States should consider appropriate measures so that persons belonging to minorities may participate fully in the economic progress and development in their country.

There is often a risk that minorities, due to their limited number compared to the majority and for other reasons, may be subjected to exclusion, marginalisation or neglect. Article 4(5) is intended to prevent these problems from happening. Similarly, minorities should not be made into museum-pieces which are required to remain on their traditional level of development while the surrounding society experiences significant improvements in their standard of living.

In the worst cases, the land areas and resources of minorities are taken over by the more powerful sectors of society, with displacement and marginalisation of the persons belonging to minorities as a consequence. In other cases, persons belonging to minorities are neglected in the economic life of the society.

Article 4(5) calls for an integration of everyone in the overall economic development of society as a whole, while ensuring that this integration takes place in ways which make it possible for the persons belonging to minorities to preserve their own identity. The balancing act required by these two separate aims can be difficult, but is facilitated by the existence of active and free associations of minorities who are fully consulted in regard to all development activities which affect or can affect their minority. Measures taken to ensure participation under Article 2 facilitate this process.

Article 5

5.1 National policies and programmes shall be planned and implemented with due regard for the legitimate interests of persons belonging to minorities.

The participation of persons belonging to minorities in the economic progress and development in their country (Art. 4(5)) can be achieved only if their interests are taken into account in the planning and implementation of national policies and programmes. Their interests go beyond purely economic aspects, however. Planning of educational policy, health policy, public nutrition policy, or housing and settlement policies are among the many aspects of social life in which the interests of the minorities should be taken into account. Only the 'legitimate' interests shall be taken into account, but the same applies to majorities: an accountable government should not promote 'illegitimate interests' from any group, whether majority or minority. The interests of minorities should be given 'due regard' which means that they should be given a reasonable weight compared to other legitimate interests with which the government is faced.

5.2 Programmes of co-operation and assistance among States should be planned and implemented with due regard for the legitimate interests of persons belonging to minorities.

This provision is of particular interest for development assistance, but relates also to other economic co-operation among states, including trade and investment agreements. There have been many instances in the past where such co-operation has neglected or directly violated the interests of minorities. Development agencies, financial institutions and others involved in international co-operation have a dual task: firstly, to ensure that legitimate interests of minorities are not negatively affected by the measures implied in the co-operation envisaged; and secondly, to ensure that persons belonging to minorities can benefit as much as members of majorities from that co-operation. The notion of 'due regard' means that a proper weight shall be given to the interests of the minorities, all factors taken into account. An assessment should be made of the likely impact of the co-operation on the affected minorities. This should be an integral part of any feasibility study.

Article 6

States should cooperate on questions relating to persons belonging to minorities, inter alia, exchanging information and experiences, in order to promote mutual understanding and confidence.

There are two sets of considerations underlying this provision. One is to share and exchange knowledge about good practices, where states can learn from each other. The other is to promote mutual understanding and confidence. The latter is of particular importance.

Situations involving minorities often have international repercussions. Tensions between states have arisen in the past and in some cases continue in the present over the treatment of minorities, particularly in the relation between the home state of a given minority and other states where persons belonging to the same ethnic, religious or linguistic group reside. Such tensions can affect the security of the countries involved and create a difficult political atmosphere both internally and internationally.

Article 6 encourages states to co-operate in order to find constructive solutions to situations involving minorities. In accordance with the Charter of the United Nations, states should observe in their bilateral relations the principle of non-intervention. They should abstain from any use of force, and also any encouragement of the use of violence by parties to group con¬flicts in other states, and take all necessary measures to prevent the incursion by any armed group or mercenaries into other states for participation in group conflicts. On the other hand, they should in their bilateral relations engage, in constructive co-operation to facilitate on a reciprocal basis, the protection of equality and promotion of group identities. One approach, much used in Central and Eastern Europe, is for States to conclude bilateral treaties or other arrangements on good neighbourly rela¬tions based on the principles of the Charter and on international human rights law, com¬bining commitments of strict non-intervention with provisions of co-operation in facili¬tating the promotion of conditions for the maintenance of group identities and transborder contacts by persons belonging to minorities. Provisions on minorities contained in such treaties and other bi¬lateral arrangements should be based on universal and regional instruments on equality, non-discrimination and minority rights. Such treaties should include provisions for the settlement of disputes over their implementation.

Article 7

States should co-operate in order to promote respect for the rights set forth in the present Declaration.

The co-operation called for in Article 7 can be undertaken at the regional and sub-regional levels as well as at the level of the United Nations. At the European level, a number of intergovernmental mechanisms and procedures have been established whose purpose at least partially is to promote in a peaceful way the right of minorities and achieve constructive group accommodation. These mechanisms include the Council of the Baltic Sea States and its Commissioner on Democratic Institutions and Human Rights, including the Rights of Persons belonging to Minorities; the OSCE region, with its office of the High Commissioner on National Minorities; and the Council of Europe which has adopted several instruments of relevance for minorities. In the United Nations, co-operation can take place through the Working Group on the Rights of Minorities.

The treaty bodies, in particular CERD, the Human Rights Committee, and the Committee on the Rights of the Child, can also have important roles to play in this regard. (See also below under Article 9)

Article 8

8.1. Nothing in the present Declaration shall prevent the fulfilment of international obligations of States in relation to persons belonging to minorities. In particular, States shall fulfil in good faith the obligations and commitments they have assumed under international treaties and agreements to which they are parties. The Declaration does not replace or modify existing international obligations in favour of persons belonging to minorities. It is an addition to, not a substitute for commitments already made.

8.2 The exercise of the rights set forth in the present Declaration shall not prejudice the enjoyment by all persons of universally recognized human rights and fundamental freedoms.

Universal human rights form the basis; the Declaration is an addition to these and intended to strengthen the implementation of human rights in regard to persons belonging to minorities but not to weaken for anyone the enjoyment of universal human rights. Consequently, the exercise of rights under the Declaration must not negatively affect the enjoyment of human rights for persons who are not persons belonging to that minority, nor for persons who belong to the minority. In their efforts to preserve the collective identity of the minority, agencies of the minority concerned cannot on the basis of Declaration adopt measures which interfere with the individual human rights of any person belonging to that minority.

8.3 Measures taken by States to ensure the effective enjoyment of the rights set forth in the present Declaration shall not prima facie be considered contrary to the principle of equality contained in the Universal Declaration of Human Rights.

Under the Universal Declaration of Human Rights Article 1, all human beings are born free and equal in dignity and rights. Under Article 2 of the Universal Declaration, everyone is entitled to all the rights set out in that declaration without distinction of any kind such as race, language, religion, or national origin. The question has been raised whether special measures in favour of national or ethnic, religious or linguistic minorities constitute a distinction in the enjoyment of human rights. It could be raised with even greater strength when taking into account the definition of racial discrimination contained in Article 1(1) of the International Convention on the Elimination of All Forms of Racial Discrimination, which reads: 'The term "racial discrimination" shall mean any distinction, exclusion, restriction or preference based on race, colour, descent, or national or ethnic origin which has the purpose or effect of nullifying or impairing the recognition, enjoyment or exercise, on an equal footing, of human rights and fundamental freedoms in the political, economic, social, cultural or any other field of public life'. The question would then be whether special measures under the Minority Declaration, which indeed would be made on 'national or ethnic origin' would constitute a preference and therefore constitute impermissible discrimination.

Article 8(3) answers this question by pointing out that such measures shall not prima facie be considered to be contrary to the principle of equality.

Under normal circumstances, measures to ensure effective participation, or ensuring that minorities benefit from economic progress in society, or have the possibility to learn their own language, will not be a privilege as compared to the other members of society. It is essential, however, that measures do not go beyond what is reasonable under the circumstances and are proportional to the aim sought to be realized.

8. 4 Nothing in the present Declaration may be construed as permitting any activity contrary to the purposes and principles of the United Nations, including sovereign equality, territorial integrity and political independence of States.

As stated in the preamble, the Declaration is based on the principles of the United Nations Charter. Note should also be taken of the conviction expressed in the preamble that the promotion and protection of rights of minorities contribute to the political and social stability of states. Article 8(4) serves as a reminder that nothing in the Declaration can be construed to permit any activity which is contrary to the purposes of the Charter. Particular mention is made of activities that are contrary to sovereign equality, territorial integrity and political independence of states. As pointed out above, the rights of persons belonging to minorities are different from the rights of peoples to self-determination, and minority rights cannot serve as a basis for claims of secession or dismemberment of the state.

Article 9

The specialized agencies and other organizations of the United Nations system shall contribute to the full realization of the rights and principles set forth in the present Declaration, within their respective fields of competence.

The different agencies and bodies of the United Nations system may in several ways contribute to the full realization of the Declaration. Projects of technical cooperation and assistance shall take the standards contained in the Declaration fully into account. The Working Group on Minorities created by the United Nations in July 1995 should serve as a stimulus for such co-operation. This Article should be seen in light of the Charter of the United Nations (Articles 55 and 56) according to which the organization shall promote respect and observance for human rights and fundamental freedoms, which now includes the rights of persons belonging to minorities. United Nations organs and specialized agencies shall give special consideration to requests for technical co-operation and assistance that are designed to achieve the aims of this Declaration.

**A POPULAR GUIDE
TO MINORITY RIGHTS
edited by
Y. N. Kly**

0-932863-19-1
$14.95 * 1995

**OUTSTANDING BOOK
on the subject of human
rights in the US, 1995**

**Gustavus Myers Center for
the Study of Human Rights**

Perhaps no other right has been so highly valued and widely sought by oppressed peoples worldwide as the right to self-determination. Yet for numerically smaller groups within multinational states, the key to achieving and sustaining equal status may lie in the possibilities afforded for collective empowerment by minority rights *in addition to civil rights.*

This is the conclusive "must-read" text for following the issues related to self-determination, minority rights and reparations so widely discussed within the American national communities today. It contains:

- Proceedings of the historic IHRAAM/Hamline University Conference on African Americans and the Right to Self-determiantion, May 14, 1993
- International minority rights texts
- Selected examples of state practice
- An easy to read Q & A on minority rights and African Americans

THE BLACK BOOK
The True Political Philosophy of Malcolm X (El Hajj Malik El Shabazz)

ISBN: 00-932863-03-5
$14.95 * 1986

Dr. Y. N. Kly is uniquely suited to edit and compile this book. As the former Chairman of the Canadian Branch of the O.A.A.U., the political organization founded by Malcolm X, Dr. Kly combines the scholarly education and international experience of a political scientist and specialist in international law with his own personal contact and instruction by Malcolm X, to produce an informative, easyoto-read analysis which epitomizes the political thought of El Hajj Malik

NOW IN ITS SEVENTH PRINTING, this highly popular book on the great African-American Muslim illustrates the influence of his Islamic faith and his international experience upon his constantly expanding political vision. The first to present a comprehensive analysis that integrates the developing vision of the man, Malcolm X, with the man he became, El Hajj Malik El Shabazz, it provides an in-depth analysis of Malcolm's directives on why the African-American struggle for national liberation and self-determination is necessary, how it should be carried on, and why it can succeed.

"Numerous works have been written on the life and ideals of Malcolm X by a marxist, liberal, communist, capitalist or Black Power follower which, obviously, paid scant regard to the total Islamic commitment of Malcolm X. Therefore, this contribution by a Muslim to clarify and analyze in depth the ideals of Malcolm X on the basis of the Qur'an and Sunnah is long overdue... Kly makes an excellent comparative study of Malcolm's ideological moorings in Islam..."

Jamalludien Ahmed Hamdulah,
***Muslim Views,* South Africa**